Children *of the* Core

KRIS L. NIELSEN

Our Children's Futures are at Risk

Children

of the

Core

What We Can Do to Fight Back

KRIS L. NIELSEN

Children of the Core

Copyright © 2013 Kris L. Nielsen

Read more at http://mgmfocus.com

For more information or to book an event,

please contact

Kris L. Nielsen by email: klnielsen74@gmail.com.

ISBN-10: 1482017741

ISBN-13: 978-1482017748

Printed in the United States of America

CONTENTS

AUTHOR'S NOTE

Throughout this book, you will see me referring to something called the "Common Core Network." I use this phrase to describe a triad of players, corporations, and institutions that are working together to dismantle public education, as we know it (Common Core proponents, the testing regime, and the privatization movement). I call it the Common Core Network because all of the components rest upon the propagation of the Common Core State Standards into all public school systems as the foundation for their collective success in unraveling democratic, locally advised, and authentic learning for our kids. As I always say, a successful institution needs a strong foundation. The network of public school devastation rests upon the foundation of the Common Core State Standards. You will see more about this in Chapter 3.

For Kathleen, my inspiration
For mom, the teacher-warrior every student deserves

For the kids, because the future still belongs to you, and we will keep fighting to make sure it's still there for you.

ACKNOWLEDGEMENTS

Honestly, I have never done this before. I've never dreamed of undertaking the monumental task of writing a book. I guess I've always considered the possibility and how nice it would be to project my voice and my thoughts to the page so that I could share with those who may find value, and that's why I love to blog. This subject is so important to me, and has such severe implications for the future, that I knew in order to put everything in one place, it had to be like this. Off I went. It quickly became completely inconceivable that I might do this on my own, so here are the people that need to be recognized for helping me, even if they didn't know of their impacts.

First, I have to thank the support and action network that has helped me get the word out and engage more people than I ever thought possible. I want to recognize Kim Parker. Without her action group, North Carolina Teachers for Change (NCTFC), my activism might never have materialized as it did. That group gave me courage and support when I felt completely alone and a little crazy. Speaking of NCTFC, I want to thank Dov Rosenburg for including me in his actions and supporting mine; Bobby Padgett and Roger Hudson, for keeping me in the loop and adding to the conversation; Donna Yates Mace, for always offering feedback and advice; Melanie Miday-Stern, for her courage and dedication; and Judy Shannon, for the moral support as I faced the Union County Board of Education with a message they didn't want to hear. Every member in that group has the courage to lead change.

My activism started from within, but was given a huge boost by the words of super-child-advocate, Lisa Michelle Nielsen, who got me thinking a little deeper about Common Core and who has been unbelievably supportive in helping me move this forward and out into the world. The inspiring activism of Peggy Robertson is a huge motivator for me; she is a superhero of change and a champion of education. My resignation from UCPS was made very public thanks to Peggy, and it launched my career as an official pain in the ass.

Also, thank you to Diane Ravitch for spreading that message even further to teachers, parents, and students who always knew something wasn't right, but thought they were alone and couldn't point to the problem. Thanks to Valerie Strauss for publishing the letter in the Washington Post, which opened it to international attention. And to Anthony Cody and Alex Russo for featuring my words on their well-known blogs.

Thanks to the Education Bloggers network for helping with advice and input and the invaluable contributions of the Opt Out Movement, and the encouragement from the following superheroes of education: Stephen Krashen, Susan Ohanian, Rosemarie Jensen, Michelle Gunderson, Robert Valiant, Kuhio Kane, Stefanie Fuhr, Shaun Johnson, Katie Osgood, Tim Slekar, Thomas Mertz, MAPS Atlanta, Jon Lubar, Glenda Blaisdell-Buck, Jenny Taylor Marshall, Karen Babcock, Athena Melville, Edy Chamness, Angie Villa, Jean Schutt McTavish, The Rebel Speducator, Claudia Swisher, Susan McEntyre, John Stoffel, Nina Bishop, Dora Taylor, Michael Goldenburg (always fiery!), Daniel Wydo, Mike Simpson, Sean Crowley, and Jonathan Massey. If even you all didn't seem to notice, your support has been invaluable. I used to try to picture what a "research team" might look like for writers of yore. Thanks goodness for Facebook friends who love to share their resources.

My drive has been boosted due to the bravery of Chris Cerrone and his colleagues in Hamburg, NY. And Danielle Boudet, who has taken on the barrage of high-stakes testing in early childhood education—your conviction lifts me.

Thanks to Aidan McCauley and Trevor Eissler for arranging my visit into the world of Montessori, where magic happens daily.

Nikhil Goyal, Stephanie Rivera, Michael Garrett, and Kayla Flynt, you are truly courageous and inspirational. Thanks for giving me the opportunity to glorify the student voice.

Thank you, Kim Cook, for allowing me to add your story and for showing the world how unfair the Common Core system is for our teachers.

Thank you, Mark Naison, for giving me permission to print your poetic words of wisdom and hope. You should be our next Secretary of Education.

Kipp Dawson, you are one of the wisest middle school educators I know. I have followed your discussions with great interest. Leonie Haimson, I am humbled by your fight and your intelligence.

I tried so hard not to forget anyone who had a place in my brain and my heart as I looked for the encouragement and material and inspiration to finish this project. If I did forget you, I'm profusely apologetic and please know that I see bravery and conviction from my colleagues around the country and the world every day. And I appreciate everything that those tireless warriors are doing. We will win. Our kids will win. Our country will thank us.

FORWARD

Last fall, Kris Nielsen's decision to resign his teaching job in North Carolina became a national sensation, because he acted on what so many classroom teachers feel every day.

But resignation is the opposite of what Nielsen is about. He quit because he refused to become resigned to what our schools are becoming. In this book he offers us an extended explanation, with his eye focused on what this means for students.

We are still on the cusp of the Common Core, and for many educators, this new set of standards has been welcomed as a relief from the oppression of high stakes tests associated with No Child Left Behind. Arne Duncan has promised that we will leave behind the narrow multiple choice tests, and that this new system will promote critical thinking, and better prepare our children for the challenges of the 21st century. Nielsen acknowledges his own initial enthusiasm – but has reached a devastating conclusion. The Common Core and the tests it will spawn are NOT a relief from the narrowing of education we endured under NCLB. They are the epitome of standardization.

Nielsen helps us see, through his deep understanding of how children learn, and by the childrens' thoughts he shares, that so long as we seek the "right answers" we are hopelessly lost. The Common Core is built upon this fundamental error. He helps us back up and reconsider what it is that our children truly need.

Ironically, Nielsen is doing the critical thinking that the Common Core falsely promised it would promote. But unlike the tests that come along to measure compliance with standards, this thinking leads us to question, to challenge, and ultimately to escape the limits of the standardized thinking that has entrapped our schools.

Anthony Cody
Living in Dialogue

"Grown-ups never understand anything by themselves, and it is tiresome for children to be always and forever explaining things to them."

- Antoine de Saint-Exupéry

PREFACE

If someone asked you what the most precious thing in your life is, how would you respond? Most parents would take no time at all in responding, "*My kids!*" I would. I'm a parent. I want what's best for my kids–I want them to be healthy, safe, and secure. I want my kids to grow up to be successful, of course, but I also want them to grow into responsible, critical, sober, creative, innovative, and productive members of our democratic society.

Sometimes, it takes a lot of trust in my society to make this happen, because I can't do it alone. Some parents try, but almost all of us need the society in which we live to help raise our children. "It takes a village..." is not just a silly buzz phrase; it's the reality. I'm lucky to live in a society where medical and scientific research and practice provide immunizations to ward off the terrible diseases of the past and treatments for the annoying ailments of today. I'm lucky to live in a society where I can simply go buy the (mostly) nutritious foods that my children need to grow and develop. I'm lucky to live in a society where my children can be exposed to tons of information with the click of a mouse, and where they can read about virtually any subject. I'm lucky to live in a society where my children can dream without limits, and actually reach those dreams, if luck and hard work are on their side.

Most of all, I'm very lucky to live in a society that believes that every child–of every background, every race, every nationality, every income level, and every ZIP code–deserves a free and strong education. And we, the citizens of this great society, are willing to pay for it, because we know we are investing in the future of our society.

So why, if we truly believe all of these things, are so many children struggling to get by in life and school? Why is it so easy to ignore those children who live in poverty and blame their schools for their inability to learn as well as their more wealthy peers?

Why are we telling our state governments that we want the cheapest, most dumbed-down, limited education we can get for our kids?

Why are we telling our state education leaders that it's okay that Timmy hates school and can't be motivated to come up with an original idea, but he can sure pass the end-of-year test like nobody's business?

Why are we telling the state governments that, even though we can't pay our teachers, buy classroom supplies, pay for field trips, invest in technology, fund scholarships, or fix our school buildings, it's okay to pay Pearson, Teach for America, ACT and College Board millions of dollars to prepare our kids for narrow, standardized tests?

Why are we telling our state governments to use our teachers and our children as pawns in field tests and other schemes that are disguised as education?

Well, of course, we're *not* telling them any of this. Why would we? We love our kids and want the best for them. The problem seems to be that we've grown so accustomed to trusting our schools to prepare our children for their futures. Trust is good. Until now.

Your kids' teachers are working so hard to make sure that they teach our children what they need to know in preparation for their futures. Many of the best teachers in the country are starting to burn out and leave the profession, however, either through attrition or early retirement. I am a part of that statistic. Why? Because I couldn't continue what I was doing knowing that the current policies in place for education are actually harming our kids.

Our schools have been quietly taken over. We are no longer teaching the skills and concepts that our kids need for the complex, unpredictable 21st century; we are increasingly teaching the skills that billionaires want their workforces to have in order to boost their profits. Gone are the days of creativity, innovation, personal growth, teamwork, and dreams; here are the days of nationalized pigeonholing, segregation, and dysfunction.

It used to be that in America, you could be whatever you dreamed you could be, and you were allowed to change your mind if your dreams led you in a new direction. In the near future, kids will be allowed to be whatever their Pearson test scores say they're qualified to be, and nothing more, unless we, their loving parents and teachers, stand up and fight for our children and their schools.

Corporate funding won't do it.

Race to the Top won't do it.

Vouchers, Teach for America, and parent trigger laws certainly won't do it.

I'm a parent first; I have been since 1994. Everything I do, think, or say has one question at its core: it this good for my children? I love my kids, just like every other parent, and I want to see them enjoy this world, get to know it, find out what makes it all work, and then become a strong and important part of it.

I became a teacher to lead, to inspire, to motivate, and to prepare kids for life. I did not become a teacher to run 175 days of test prep for constant benchmark testing and one big assessment at the end of the year, and that's certainly not why any of us send our kids to school each day. Let me tell you a story.

In 2008, I spoke to my assistant principal about my students' state test scores, just after my first, full-year teaching assignment at an Albuquerque middle school. It was my first discussion of that type and my first summative evaluation by a supervisor. I taught science to eager and curious 6th graders—a group that had not yet been jaded by lectures, vocabulary quizzes, study guides, and multiple-choice tests—and I was a little nervous to hear how administration felt about my mostly student-led and hands-on approach to teaching and learning.

At the end of the year, my students had taken their state standardized assessments in science, math, and reading and the initial results had come to us within weeks. The New Mexico Standards-Based Assessments, as they were called, are blended tests, made up of multiple-choice, short answer, and essay questions. They take students a week to finish and weeks to months to score. The scores did not directly affect any teacher's job, but they were used as handy *informal* evaluation tools during meetings like the one I was in.

My supervisor made my evaluation sound ominous by sighing heavily as she pulled data tables and graphs out of a manila file folder, laid them beside my professional development plan (PDP) documents, and looked at me with raised eyebrows.

"I need you to tell me something, Kris," she said, "I have some questions that I'd like you to answer." (This, incidentally, is the best way of which I can think for an administrator to loosen the bladder of a new teacher. It almost worked.)

She showed me the data in the graphs, which showed my students scoring 15% or higher than all other 6th grade students— in all subjects. I relaxed and smiled tentatively, since my supervisor still had her eyebrows raised and she still wasn't smiling. She wanted to know *how*, she wanted to know *why*, and she most of all wanted to know *what the difference was* between my peers and me.

Still a little shaky from my initial scare, I began to speak as eloquently as possible about my tendency toward discovery learning, problem- and project-based learning, student-centered study, use of technology, and performance assessment. I also explained that our school's policy encouraging student-led parent conferences really boosted my students' and parents' engagement and attention as they prepared for those presentations. I felt a little like I was babbling when she stopped me suddenly with a very difficult question.

"Why do you think the other teachers aren't doing this?"

She caught me totally off guard and I had no immediate answer. Again, with the raised eyebrow, she was waiting for some words of wisdom, or at least a semi-plausible answer that she could turn into action. I didn't have that answer at the ready. I hadn't seen other teachers in action (it hadn't occurred to me at that point that observing other teachers was so important to *my* development), and all of the things happening in my classroom were just natural, I supposed. In my world, I didn't understand why anyone *wouldn't* be doing those things. It was the difference between boring and fun, and I already knew that boring didn't lead to learning.

Finally, my reply was almost a question in itself: "Because it's hard?"

I remember that meeting so vividly because it's the moment that my realization of public school woes and my dedication to changing those woes into successes met face to face. I was a brand new teacher and knew that I was relatively powerless, but one of the beautiful things about being a teacher is the ability to make changes in my own realm. That was my mission from that point forward: to create meaningful change in my own classroom that led students to success.

My mission has taken several turns as I've sought the perfect balance between skills and concepts and applications and critical thinking and the rest of the cornucopia of things I want my students to be able to master. Often, I've found myself focusing too much on one thing and have had to build up focus on other things. Every year brought a new personal initiative that I wanted to try—from inquiry to games, from writing to technology—but without ever sacrificing the previous years' work. The result grew into a conglomeration of it all. I've shared and I've taken ideas from not only my school-building colleagues, but my global colleagues, as well (having a global network of people to learn from is incredibly important). I've collected formal and informal data along the way, which helps me to determine what stays and what goes. And I've listened.

One of the most challenging things to master for a professional teacher, who works in relative isolation, is *listening*. We generally live and work in one room, with several young humans, planning and executing our own lessons. We speak, we question, we teach. We do listen to our students, of course, but we don't often listen—*really* listen—to colleagues and supervisors and parents. We are a proud bunch and we like to think that our shortcomings are minor and individually surmountable. We tend to get a little defensive when something we do well, in our own minds, is questioned or critiqued. It's difficult to step out of our comfort zones (our classroom world) and become part of a community. Many teachers report being the most uncomfortable when colleagues enter their classrooms to observe, as if the comfort zone has somehow been violated.

It wasn't easy for me, either. It was nerve-wracking and uncomfortable allowing myself to open up to the scrutiny of others. It got to a point, however, that continued isolation from the rest of the profession began to weigh on me. I started to feel the beginnings of that dreaded teacher malady: burnout. I'm now a firm believer that the immunization to teacher burnout is collaboration and communication.

I've invited parents, colleagues, and administrators from around the district to see the things happening in my classroom and then provide me with feedback on what they observed. I've also videotaped lessons and made them publicly available for feedback. Again, it was terrifying at first, but that feedback was the most important element in my ongoing experimentation in the middle school classroom. And that feedback was all over the place.

Many teachers were in tune with what I was doing and gave me new ideas and used my ideas. Some teachers smiled and watched and then left without saying anything. I would often hear later through the grapevine that these teachers simply didn't agree with certain aspects of the lesson, or any of it. Some didn't like the noise or the student-led structure, or wondered where the traditional methods went. Some wondered how I expected the students to learn anything if I didn't lead every lesson with a lecture. I always wished I could talk more with teachers like that, since I know we could have learned a lot from each other.

Feedback from administrators had been just as varied—from the praise and the school-wide implementation of my ideas to utter disagreements and warnings (I had a principal tell me to stop using pop culture in my math classes since it didn't help students score higher on tests). One administrator asked me to present the promise of a new math curriculum to parents after observing my use of problem-based instruction; many parents are not supportive of this newer form of learning and apparently need to be "sold."

And then there were the students. Here is one type of feedback that teachers and parents tend to push aside and I want to impress upon all of us how big of a mistake that is. Kids are honest when they know their opinions are valued and they will provide surprisingly useful judgments. If an adult has an open mind, it's impossible to underestimate the power of student feedback. We need to listen to these kids; they know when they're learning and when they're not.

So, back to my summative evaluation in 2008. My answer to the question, "Why do you think the other teachers aren't doing this?" was right: it *is* hard. It is more difficult to make sure that every lesson or task is student-led, constructivist, collaborative, literacy-geared, problem-based, inquiry-led, and assessed with meaningful and impactful feedback. The good news is it doesn't have to be—and it's what our kids need and want. The results and rewards are amazing, and real learning takes place.

The bad news is that the American school system, since 2002, is designed to punish teachers and students who attempt to take an authentic path to learning. The system has been taken over, and our kids have become commodities that are being traded and sold and ranked and filed among the wealthy corporate elite that now attempts to control their futures. It didn't seem to be that difficult for them, unfortunately, and there's a reason for that.

My generation, and any generation before me, is trained to gauge success and learning through percentages and averages.

My students today have parents who want to know what their children scored or how their work compares to the class average. We are so used to being competitive against and compared to each other. We have to move away from this paradigm. It just won't work anymore, not in the rapidly changing times in which we live. I want to see students (and parents) move away from that arbitrary and limited feedback and into more authentic, individualized feedback—the stuff that makes them part of the real world and really makes them proud.

There were a few critical things missing from the beginning of my career, without which I believe made my efforts more successful and made my students feel proud, productive, and part of something bigger. There were no Common Core State Standards. There were no benchmark tests every 6 weeks. There were not yet the official one-size-fits-all models of teaching and learning, where every student in the grade level was expected to learn the exact same thing at the exact same time and were tested constantly to see if everyone was proficient before moving on. My supervisor didn't have to tie student scores to my job performance, because that would be unscientific and unethical.

There were no field tests that wasted my time or precious learning time for my students. There were threats of sanctions against the schools for not making adequate yearly progress (AYP), but at least we were able to band together to make a collaborative difference using our own collective expertise. Finally, our funding wasn't based on adhering to national standards and Federal rules—our state and district were allowed to determine what was best for our local demographic.

Everybody in this country has a very real and very serious stake in what happens to education in this country. The future of our economy, our democracy, our national security, and our place in the global community depends on it. Parents have a very important stake in this because these are our children, who we trust every day to a system that has turned its back on them and their teachers.

I think most people have heard of the Common Core State Standards, but aren't truly aware of what they really mean or what the threat is.

I wrote this book to help bring awareness to a new attack on our kids and our country by three teams of wolves that are wrapped in sheep's clothing: the architects of the Common Core State Standards, the standardized testing regime that accompanies it, and the privatization movement that closes "failing" schools and sells them to charter operators. I've seen this assault on our kids clearly for three years, although I know it's been going on for much longer. I want others to see what's hiding behind the curtains of pretty language and inspirational propaganda of the proponents of the Common Core State Standards. Digging just a little deeper reveals a very ugly, very bleak attempt to pigeonhole our children and limit their potentials just to advance profits and rank students for some planned, future idea of a workforce. Innovation, creativity, and good paying jobs will be reserved for the top (most affluent) students; long hours, low pay, and menial work will be prescribed for the bottom (poorest) students. And it will all be based on how they perform on state standardized tests, which are designed to be very closely matched to—you guessed it—the Common Core State Standards.

This has to be the start of a new movement, of which parents are a critical part. We need students to not only perform, but also think and produce. We need students to start reaching out to an audience bigger than the four walls of a classroom and to start collaborating with others outside of the boundaries of the school. And when they do, they should expect deep, meaningful feedback from us that will alter the way they view themselves and their work, rather than shallow percentages and scores. I want students to know that they are not just trying to pass school, but are participants of the huge coalition of thinkers on this planet. This is the beginning of the training that the world expects them to have and the start of the promise of a better life.

Teachers and administrators should expect no less of themselves, either. Teachers in isolation are still too common and increasingly problematic. To ready students for the global age of learning and competing, it makes no sense that teachers use limited resources and take part in occasional collaboration with team members or colleagues. We—parents and teachers— are the guidance system of the 21st century American culture and we should be preparing ourselves in earnest as well. If that sounds too grandiose for our titles and our jobs, then go back and revisit the reasons you became a parent or a teacher in the first place. I think that will change your stance.

Administrators and district leaders need to revisit their roles and their relationships to teachers and students, and they should understand the power of feedback in relation to their jobs—not just raw, numerical data, but real, authentic, meaningful feedback. Micromanagement of teachers has also become a real problem, and it is felt throughout the school.

My own journey—as a student, a teacher, and a parent—through the American educational system so far has been many things: enlightening, fun, frustrating, demoralizing, intense, adventurous, inspiring and hilarious; it's been a test of endurance and an insightful look at the big picture, which brings me to share the information in these pages. I've seen great people doing amazing things for our kids. I've seen great people doing not-so-amazing things for our kids. I've seen a few people who shouldn't be involved in education at all. I've worked under standards in three states, the Common Core State Standards Initiative in two states, and have studied many other states' standards and systems. I've researched and used several different curriculum resources in all content areas. Both my undergraduate and graduate degrees are in education, with a strong emphasis on curriculum, instruction, and child development. After observing and talking and writing and presenting and teaching through all of it, I have this to say: all of us need to start using our greatest resource more positively and consistently; that resource is *people*. We need to stop acting alone and start making a change. America has had its educational problems for a while, but this new "reform" movement, propped up by the Common Core State Standards Initiative is taking us in the opposite direction that we need to go, and is doing damage that may someday be irreparable.

Thank you for taking the time to consider my ideas as you read; and thank you, on behalf of our kids and our country, for taking the first steps to shaking things up a bit and making the changes that the new century calls on us to make. If the United States is to remain competitive on the world stage, we must once again become among the world's great innovators and thinkers.

If this is our hope, then it is the full responsibility of today's parents, students, educators to guide the next generation into preparation for those important roles. We can accomplish this by overthrowing this growing coup and leading a new public school movement that will serve all of our kids, without churning out standardized, assembly-line children.

INTRODUCTION

The Need for Change

"Standardization of our educational systems is apt to stamp out individualism and defeat the very ends of education by leveling the product down rather than up."
- Harvey Cushing

In the introductions of many books about the state of American education, there are lengthy discussions about the miseries, the shortcomings, and the dismal future we have put before our children. The trends and the statistics are troubling and there doesn't seem to be an easy fix. We lag behind other developed and industrial nations in math and science. We dread the future of the next generation, which seems completely engrossed in and allegiant to their video games and Facebook and text messaging. There are so many things that make the future look bleak for our nation and its educational system. The message always seems to be, "We're doomed!"

So far, however, we haven't found a magic wand or perfect pill to create the transformations we desire, regardless of the countless hours of debate, discussions, and outright fighting to fix our nation's schools. What we have created, so far, is a discourse that always seeks to blame some person or some group of educators or parents for the perceived achievement shortcomings, while leaving our nation's children behind as they wait for us to fix the problem.

This book will reverse that discussion, because this conversation should be about our kids, and only about our kids, and because the underlying cause of the dismal failures we continue to see is grounded in the same movement that is trying to convince us that help is on the way. In fact, one overall message in this book will be how propaganda and corporate interest have guided us into a tangled web of scapegoating, diversions, self-interest, and misinformation; and how the long road to freedom from this web is littered with the stories of activist students, teachers, parents, and others. I am a character in one of those stories.

In the Fall of 2012, I resigned my position as a science teacher with Union County Public Schools in North Carolina. The reason for the resignation was health-related concerns that had begun to pile up. The reason I wrote the resignation letter that circled the globe in less than a week was to expose hidden and serious circumstances that plague almost every teacher and every student, every day. Here is the letter, in its original form, as posted on the United Opt Out website[1]:

October 25, 2012

To All it May Concern:

I'm doing something I thought I would never do—something that will make me a statistic and a caricature of the times. Some will support me, some will shake their heads and smirk condescendingly—and others will try to convince me that I'm part of the problem. Perhaps they're right, but I don't think so. All I know is that I've hit a wall, and in order to preserve my sanity, my family, and the forward movement of our lives, I have no other choice.

Before I go too much into my choice, I must say that I have the advantages and disadvantages of differentiated experience under my belt. I have seen the other side, where the grass was greener, and I unknowingly jumped the fence to where the foliage is either so tangled and dense that I can't make sense of it, or the grass is wilted and dying (with no true custodian of its health). Are you lost? I'm talking about public K-12 education in North Carolina. I'm talking about my history as a successful teacher and leader in two states before moving here out of desperation.

In New Mexico, I led a team of underpaid teachers who were passionate about their jobs and who did amazing things. We were happy because our students were well behaved, our community was supportive, and our jobs afforded us the luxuries of time, respect, and visionary leadership. Our district was huge, but we got things done because we were a team. I moved to Oregon because I was offered a fantastic job with a higher salary, a great math program, and superior benefits for my family. Again, I was given the autonomy I dreamed of, and I used it to find new and risky ways to introduce technology into the math curriculum. My peers looked forward to learning from me, the community gave me a lot of money to get my projects off the ground, and my students were amazing.

Then, the bottom fell out. I don't know who to blame for the budget crisis in Oregon, but I know it decimated the educational coffers. I lost my job only due to my lack of seniority. I was devastated. My students and their parents were angry and sad. I told myself I would hang in there, find a temporary job, and wait for the recall. Neither the temporary job nor the recall happened. I tried very hard to keep my family in Oregon—applying for jobs in every district, college, private school, and even Toys R Us. Nothing happened after over 300 applications and 2 interviews.

The Internet told me that the West Coast was not hiring teachers anymore, but the East Coast was the go-to place. Charlotte, North Carolina couldn't keep up with the demand! I applied with three schools, got three phone interviews, and was even hired over the phone. My very supportive and adventurous family and I packed quickly and moved across the country, just so I could keep teaching.

I had come from two very successful and fun teaching jobs to a new state where everything was different. During my orientation, I noticed immediately that these people weren't happy to see us; they were much more interested in making sure we knew their rules. It was a one-hour lecture about what happens when teachers mess up. I had a bad feeling about teaching here from the start; but, we were here and we had to make the best of it.

Union County seemed to be the answer to all of my problems. The rumors and the press made it sound like UCPS was the place to be progressive, risky, and happy. So I transferred from CMS to UCPS. They made me feel more welcome, but it was still a mistake to come here.

Let me cut to the chase: I quit. I am resigning my position as a teacher in the state of North Carolina—

permanently. I am quitting without notice (taking advantage of the "at will" employment policies of this state). I am quitting without remorse and without second thoughts. I quit. I quit. I quit!

Why?

Because...

I refuse to be led by a top-down hierarchy that is completely detached from the classrooms for which it is supposed to be responsible.

I will not spend another day under the expectations that I prepare every student for the increasing numbers of meaningless tests.

I refuse to be an unpaid administrator of field tests that take advantage of children for the sake of profit.

I will not spend another day wishing I had some time to plan my fantastic lessons because administration comes up with new and inventive ways to steal that time, under the guise of PLC meetings or whatever. I've seen successful PLC development. It doesn't look like this.

I will not spend another day wondering what menial, administrative task I will hear that I forgot to do next. I'm far enough behind in my own work.

I will not spend another day wondering how I can have classes that are full inclusion, and where 50% of my students have IEPs, yet I'm given no support.

I will not spend another day in a district where my coworkers are both on autopilot and in survival mode. Misery loves company, but I will not be that company.

I refuse to subject students to every ridiculous standardized test that the state and/or district thinks is important. I refuse to have my higher-level and deep-thinking lessons disrupted by meaningless assessments (like the EXPLORE test) that do little more than increase stress among children and teachers, and attempt to guide young adolescents into narrow choices.

I totally object and refuse to have my performance as an educator rely on "Standard 6." It is unfair, biased, and does not reflect anything about the teaching practices of proven educators.

I refuse to hear again that it's more important that I serve as a test administrator than a leader of my peers.

I refuse to watch my students being treated like prisoners. There are other ways. It's a shame that we don't have the vision to seek out those alternatives.

I refuse to watch my coworkers being treated like untrustworthy slackers through the overbearing policies of this state, although they are the hardest working and most overloaded people I know.

I refuse to watch my family struggle financially as I work in a job to which I have invested 6 long years of my life in preparation. I have a graduate degree and a track record of strong success, yet I'm paid less than many two-year degree holders. And forget benefits— they are effectively nonexistent for teachers in North Carolina.

I refuse to watch my district's leadership tell us about the bad news and horrific changes coming towards us, then watch them shrug incompetently, and then tell us to work harder.

I refuse to listen to our highly regarded superintendent telling us that the charter school movement is at our doorstep (with a soon-to-be-elected governor in full support) and tell us not to worry about it, because we are applying for a grant from Race to the Top. There is no consistency here; there is no leadership here.

I refuse to watch my students slouch under the weight of a system that expects them to perform well on EOG tests, which do not measure their abilities other than memorization and application and therefore do not measure their readiness for the next grade level—much less life, career, or college.

I'm tired of watching my students produce amazing things, which show their true understanding of 21st century skills, only to see their looks of disappointment when they don't meet the arbitrary expectations of low-level state and district tests that do not assess their skills.

I refuse to hear any more about how important it is to differentiate our instruction as we prepare our kids for tests that are anything but differentiated. This negates our hard work and makes us look bad.

I am tired of hearing about the miracles my peers are expected to perform, and watching the districts do next to nothing to support or develop them. I haven't seen real professional development in either district since I got here. The development sessions I have seen are sloppy, shallow, and have no real means of evaluation or accountability.

I'm tired of my increasing and troublesome physical symptoms that come from all this frustration, stress, and sadness.

Finally, I'm tired of watching parents being tricked into believing that their children are being prepared for the complex world ahead, especially since their children's teachers are being cowed into meeting expectations and standards that are not conducive to their children's futures.

I'm truly angry that parents put so much stress, fear, and anticipation into their kids' heads in preparation for the EOG tests and the new MSLs—neither of which are consequential to their future needs. As a parent of a high school student in Union County, I'm dismayed at the education that my child receives, as her teachers frantically prepare her for more tests. My toddler will not attend a North Carolina public school. I will do whatever it takes to keep that from happening.

I quit because I'm tired being part of the problem. It's killing me and it's not doing anyone else any good. Farewell.

My main message was: it shouldn't be this way. There is a better way; there are many better ways. After the publicity and discussions started to wane, and with the help of my friends, I continued to feed the discussions that might move our schools back to being the academic and community centers that we should expect them to be. I went from being a teacher to a parent activist. It was liberating, as well as frightening. Over the next several months, I realized I wasn't alone. There is a growing network of us, trying our best to save what we know is the most important thing: a democratic and progressive education for our kids.

"Inside-out" change means that the frontline educators and parents, and those in direct contact with students (and sometimes, the students themselves), know better than anyone else what works and what doesn't when it comes to student achievement and real learning. And it's the ultimate goal of this book to mobilize those frontline specialists into forming the basis of the movement that will transform education in this country.

It's time for educators and parents (not politicians or corporations) to once again lead the charge.

Just as important, I hope to engage parents in a deeper conversation about how their students are being taught and cared for in our schools, and how to be better advocates for their students and teachers. Parents are the key to true change that impacts students. Without our parents, we are standing on a three-legged stool, which is missing a leg. Groups like Parent Revolution and StudentsFirst (with their very ironic and misleading names) have made many attempts to disjoint the connection between teachers, parents, and students. Only with the trio that holds the stool up can students—and our schools and our nation—stay strong and progressive.

It's important to know that one person can't do this alone. I caused a wave to move through the system with my resignation, and other brave educators work tirelessly by speaking up, speaking out, and pushing for change. People listened, but this isn't how the change is going to happen. This is going to take numbers. It's going to take a concerted effort among thousands—maybe millions—of citizens ready to defend our country and the promise of our kids' futures by refusing to participate in destructive policy and discourse.

Why the Common Core is Dangerous

The public schools have been blamed for killing creativity and motivation in young people for some time, setting up the inevitability of future high school dropouts, and cursing high-energy preadolescents with sedentary learning without recess or play. The sad truth is that all of these complaints have some merit in the majority of schools and the new system is making it much, much worse, especially in low-income, urban and rural schools.

In a recent editorial written by 14 year-old student, Line Dalile, the public school experience is clearly summed up: "You learned to stop questioning the world, to go with the flow, and that there's only one right answer to each question.[2]" This quote describes what it feels like to be in a classroom led by one-size-fits-all policies. No Child Left Behind (NCLB) kicked this into high gear; the Obama Administration's Race to the Top (RttT) initiative to get school districts and states to compete for federal funds, using standardized tests as the measure of success, will cause students like Line to do one of two things: conform or leave. The United States continues to create and fund measures that are moving us in the wrong direction amid a world that is becoming ever more innovative and collectively competitive around us. The kids seem to know it intuitively, while the adults seem to stand in denial.

Competition is what drives a capitalist society. Competition drives the need to be the best, to outperform the other groups who play in the same game, and to rise above the rest and be recognized. When the private sector operates under these principles (and when the system works as it should), these ideas work well for all. Corporations and businesses enjoy growth and profit, consumers enjoy lower prices and plenty of choice, the government sees higher tax revenues and balanced budgets, and the population as a whole sees a well-rounded civilization that works.

Competition also drives educational achievement, but this should be done in a different way. Traditionally, it has always been "every man for himself" in terms of getting the best grades, scoring the highest percentile on tests, and getting into the best colleges. That type of competition will never go away, but there are some important changes that must be considered, which are happening within the global economy, and successful U.S. corporate leaders are strongly aware of how their workforces must look in order to stay competitive with the rest of the industrial world. Educators must also be aware of these changes and be willing and able to modify their instructional programs to meet the needs of an evolving American economy.

Unfortunately, the American political system is stuck in the old ways of driving competition. No Child Left Behind and Race to the Top have emphasized standardized assessments as the focus of determining student learning and ranking, much to the dismay of teachers and students alike. Also, as districts and states compete against each other for funding, it makes the nation as a whole educationally weaker. Federal programs like these are inherently biased toward schools with predominantly higher socioeconomic status and fewer minority students. Those schools that do not compete or, rather, *cannot* compete do not receive funding and are at risk of corrective action, up to and including school closings. There are several damaging effects of this type of legislation, and the focus of this book is the effect on the futures of students in terms of livelihood and readiness and the future of our country in the growing world economy.

According to the 2011 Workforce Readiness Report Card (an annual publication from a consortium of educational and corporate researchers compiled from survey data from over 400 employers), deficiencies are prevalent in high school graduates in both academic and applied skills that corporations value highly. When employers are surveyed every year, they rank the importance of certain skills—both basic knowledge and applied skills—as they apply to respective educational attainment levels (high school, two-year degree, and four-year degree). The report card also presents the skills those employers observe as lacking in students of those attainment levels.

Several studies have focused on skills that should be included in every school curriculum and made part of every content class. There are teachers and leaders who recognize this vital need and they do implement these skills in every lesson. The top five applied skills necessary for job success for new workforce entrants are, in order of most to least importance are:

1. Professionalism
2. Collaboration
3. Oral Communications
4. Critical Thinking
5. Written Communications

According to the report, over half of employers believe that high school graduates are deficient in all but collaboration.[3]

Although most educational experts will agree that these five skills should be part of the educational preparation of young citizens, U.S. public schools are currently choked with the expectations of meeting mostly ambiguous adequate yearly progress (AYP) goals, showing high growth, and reaching arbitrary academic objectives—as prescribed by No Child Left Behind and state boards of education—in only two areas: mathematics and reading. Our schools have restricted learning to focus on those two subjects at the expense of all others. Teachers complain about the loss of creativity, innovation, and authentic learning; principals are closing arts and physical education programs in order to make room for interventions ordered by corrective actions. And students are exhausted, bored, and checking out.

Our current, traditional school experience doesn't lead to learning; it leads to high-school dropouts and stressed-out kids. That's right: competition drives ultimate failure for too many of our kids. It has to. That's how the system is defined—a few winners outrunning a majority of losers. This has nothing to do with "kids these days," since it's always been this way, we just have higher stakes and more toxic environments now. This is a dangerous way to lead America into the new global economy.

If we are going to be data-driven, let's start with data from the real world and change the data instruments in our school buildings to meet the demands of the global knowledge economy, releasing ourselves from the demands of for-profit, end-of-grade-focused schools, companies, and governments. This is about student success and readiness in a democratic society, and it cannot be all about "racing to the top" to see who gets the biggest prize. We should be assisting each other to the finish line, instead of tripping over ourselves to beat each other, and we should be teaching our students to do the same. We should be working together.

This book will discuss in detail the justification to lead students into a new type of competition, which will require every American citizen collaborating and celebrating together. Instead of the "every man for himself" variety of competition, our goal will be leading students to thrive in the "every person for the team" model. We have to start changing our *middle* schools, not *high* schools, to prepare students to become the adults they want and need to be. That looks much different from what many people might think—it certainly looks different from what we're seeing in classrooms now.

Teaching is a research-based, yet heart-driven practice, based on many types of informal and formal qualitative and quantitative data, and it's getting more complex. The Common Core State Standards were designed to standardize teaching and learning, measure that learning using low-level and very expensive tests to derive one type of data, and then show the poor results as reason to hand public schools to private companies that wish to invest in their turnaround.

Unfortunately, "turnaround," in this case, is a misnomer. Instead of investing in real student learning, the privatizers are fully invested in raising test scores to show proficiency of students and schools, which leads to more funding from the Federal "Race to the Top" initiative. That's the deal. That's the plan. Nothing more. This is what I call the "Common Core Network."

American educators and administrators are stuck in the power play happening between publishing and assessment companies, the politicians who enable them through lawmaking, and the privatizers who wrote and are investing in the Common Core State Standards as the foundation of this corruption. These people aren't education specialists and they aren't (usually) educators. Even the Common Core State Standards were authored by two lawyers, one of whom is David Coleman (the new CEO of College Board)[4]. Their friends are businesspeople who are concerned with making a profit by raising test scores using their products and getting their brands into the classroom door, behind which lies a multibillion dollar prize. These are billionaires looking to cash in on their investments by causing public schools to fail so that they can replace them with private charters. Cronyism is alive and kicking in the arena of K-12 education.

Burying low-income and minority public schools under the profiteering schemes will not prepare students for the future; it will have the opposite effect. And carving the country up by class will not bolster our economy or our society; it will bankrupt us and destroy our way of life as we know it. The Common Core State Standards Initiative is the nationalization of public education that corporate reformers need to make this happen.

There is, thankfully, a large team of specialists who have the energy, the drive, the ambition, and the experience to reform our schools the way they need to be reformed. That team should be moving us forward with the know-how that our students need and deserve. That team is made up of the millions of students and teachers and parents in this country who are increasingly finding themselves in the positions at the front lines of the battle to save our kids and their schools.

It's time to revisit our school policies to prepare our students for high school, for college, for work, and for life. Since we've seen that the "top-down" corporate-hierarchical model hasn't worked and will not work, let's start from the bottom up. Let's use our tried-and-true collective expertise to make a real difference in the lives of our students. Teachers got into teaching for this reason; it's time to stand up, take it all back, and make it count. They need our help.

But first, let's take a look at our students' expectations and needs from the adults in their lives.

Children of the Core

1

What They Need From Us

"Educationists should build the capacities of inquiry, creativity, entrepreneurial and moral leadership among students, and become their role models."

- Abdul Kalam

Kids are truly amazing little creatures, and I mean that seriously. As a huge fan of George Carlin, I laugh to tears at much of his material and even use some of it to put humor into my activism. I remember watching one special where he spent some time ranting that our kids aren't special—some are goofy-looking, some are clumsy, some are smelly, etc.—and I don't think I ever laughed at that part. Not because it wasn't funny, it was (let's face it, many kids are those things); it's just that I find young humans so fascinating! All of them. From birth to adulthood, kids are very interesting if you pay attention. They're clumsy, they're loud, and they're messy; they're also determined, tireless, and devoted to the task at hand.

What impresses me the most is the way their minds work. A newborn infant comes into this world ready to attempt two things: survive and *learn*. They never get tired of it! Kids, from birth, are always learning, and they get better and better at it as they grow. Our children are inherently curious and, as the quote from Line Dalile suggested in the introduction, it takes school to kill that curiosity and that inherent love of learning. If you want to point to one thing and call it an "educational crisis," that should be it.

As kids grow towards adulthood, they start to think more abstractly and in a more controlled and focused way. One of the great achievements in any child's life is that ability to transition from concrete to abstract thinking, and it is this transition that allows children to become truly innovative adults and contributory citizens to the progress of their communities. To reduce their expectations of important feedback from the natural world to rote memorization and simple feedback is stifling and frustrating to their development.

If you ask a group of teachers to go back in time a little bit, to when they were all brand new and green, they will agree that there was one thing on their minds: *making a difference*. Those three words may have meant many different things for many different teachers, but the sentiment is the same. We want to make a difference in kids' lives. That passion lingers because it's what we all believe in. But how many times does a teacher now get sidetracked from that mission to make time for meeting paperwork deadlines and making sure that her students are geared up, practiced, and in solid form for the upcoming high-stakes state assessments?

Our students need us all to be leaders and advocates for their futures. This sounds automatic and relatively easy, but anyone who's spent any amount of time following education news knows that there are challenges and roadblocks along the way. This is going to take commitment and courage and dedication and hard work. Most importantly, we're being forced to do it wrong and it needs to change.

Our kids have expectations of the adults in their lives. Here are the things they need from us.

They Need Us to Understand Them

A coworker of mine summed up perfectly the issue of classroom management in middle school: "If you treat them like babies, they will act like babies." I believe the logic then dictates that if we treat them as people we respect and trust, and then they will behave as respectful and trustworthy people.

After performing a Google search for, "what makes a great teacher?" an exhausting list of articles from teachers, specialists, and academics pops up. Interspersed among them is the occasional article where a student survey was performed and analyzed. The differences between the two types of article are obvious right away. Almost every teacher or education specialist will point to "high expectations" as the most important characteristic of great teachers, and I tentatively agree. When you hold all students to the same high expectations to perform, they know where you want them to be and that you expect them to get there without accepted anything less. However, the number one aspect of a great teacher according to students is the ability to get to know them and make them feel important as individuals.

This isn't just students talking. There is growing evidence that suggests that when students feel that their teachers know them personally (and aren't afraid to share a little bit of personal information themselves), those students do perform higher in class and with more dedication. Dr. Robert Marzano, of the Marzano Research Laboratory, is one of those researchers and an advocate of building relationships with students. According to Dr. Marzano, we don't have to be their friends, but we do need to be people that they trust and value in their lives, and they need to understand that we feel the same about them.[1]

Teachers have to get to know their students—not just as individual data points (as we are told to by the policies of Race to the Top), but also as individual human beings. We should know what they love, what they fear, what they're interested in, and what bores them. We should get to know their social circles and their styles of interaction, and get to know their families and how they spend time at home. This sounds like a lot of work—and it is, thanks to the budget cuts that have ballooned our class sizes. But it's worth it when you realize the benefits that come from it for the rest of the year. When students feel that they have a positive relationship with their teachers, they will do almost anything for that teacher, including hard work.

These important relationships have taken a slide in priority with the growing focus on standardized testing achievement. There are more and more teachers who feel that building relationships with their students is a fringe duty that doesn't compete with building basic skills. Not only do these teachers end up seeing the blowback of this assumption with undesirable behavior and even negative impact on achievement, but also most teacher evaluations look for the ability of teachers to create environments that are respectful of student differences and abilities. The ability to take the time to foster those relationships will cover all of those bases, and it will make teachers feel great about the things they're doing for our kids. When students are reduced to scores and ranks, relationships become less important, and students notice.

They Need Us to Encourage Them

The most heartbreaking experiences I've had over the years were when a few students who had achieved so highly and proudly all year were deflated after receiving their lower-than-expected scores on end-of-year standardized tests. Why do we allow this? Imagine being the student who has been engaged, productive, motivated, and proud for an entire year, only to be downgraded by a percentile and a scale score.

Encouragement is a powerful instrument in educator and parent toolkits. It doesn't always have to be praise and pats on the back; in fact, the most effective encouragement is usually of the "try one more time" variety. This means giving students meaningful feedback from which they can grow and continue to learn.

Percentages on tests and averages in class provide neither meaningful feedback nor encouragement—they deliver little more a final message. Either you passed or you failed, neither of which will encourage a student to try harder or push their own limits.

One approach to providing better feedback is the rubric, which any teacher who uses understanding by design (UbD) knows how to use and has used many times. Starting with the end in mind is made easier when a rubric for assessment is created. This practice is a pragmatic way for teachers to make sure that learning is happening and that the objectives of the unit are met while it's all happening. Many teachers claim success with this format of instructional design. The point here is that there are better ways to assess learning, which also continue the learning past some final score.

A major theme that has come from research and practice (including my own) is the effectiveness of intrinsic vs. extrinsic motivation types. It's common sense that everyone needs some sort of motivation to do the things they do every day. If we go to work, it's because we love doing the work we do (intrinsic) or it's because we can't live without the paycheck (extrinsic), or both. If we clean the house it's because it feels good to live in a tidy environment (intrinsic) or it's because we're tired of tripping over our possessions (extrinsic). If we want kids to go to school, there has to be a motivation for them, preferably of the intrinsic type.

In most schools, the motivation is automatically extrinsic, because we think that the best way to get kids to perform is to motivate them with high grades, prizes, recognition, or (inversely) punish them for not doing well by taking away privileges, making them repeat a grade, or pushing them into tutoring. My research during my master's program showed that intrinsic motivation was much more effective in getting students to work hard, complete projects, and even show up to class every day. Surveys showed that students would rather feel good about their products than receive high grades, and they would prefer to get honest and constructive feedback from teachers than receive grades that determined where they fit on a continuum. They would also much rather not do their work than risk failure, and this fact is a failure of *our* policies and ideas.

Failure has been historically contrasted to success as its opposite—when you fail, you have not succeeded, and that's that. Apparently, NASA's Gene Kranz never actually said, "failure is not an option" when Apollo 13 was in trouble, but the phrase has been adopted as part of an anti-education buzz lately. The trend among social educator networks is that failure should not only be an option, but even a requirement, since the perseverance to rebound from failure leads to strong achievement. Perhaps a middle ground is in order.

In any case, failure should never be the end result of a process of learning. The term "failure" should, in all frankness, leave our lexicon forever, since what we should offer kids is a way to review, revise, and redo—without the fear of failing. Let's make sure that our students are trained to recognize failure as the prompt to try again, to try a little harder, and to revise the work in which they did not show proficiency. Failure should never be the opposite of success; it should be a stepping-stone toward success.

They Need Us to Include Them

There is a growing awareness and concern that we've been pushing so hard with our numerous agendas and initiatives and toward our adult objectives and goals (many of those, it turns out, are not very conducive to student learning) and we've been trained very well to recognize achievement as a scale score. And we've been doing this for the past decade without the student voice. We've been hardliners in the ideology that the adults know best and the students need to respect that. In the meantime, we've seen a rise in dropout rates, behavior problems, and bullying. Obviously, we can't blame ourselves for all of this, but we can start to remove our focus from the end game and start to pay better attention to the issues that students can help us solve.

A new movement needs to rise where the student voice is equally participant in the discussions of all things education, from policy to instruction to teacher evaluation. Like I mentioned before, students give honest answers when they know their words are valued, and I believe that there is real value in considering student voices beyond what we've ever done before. There are some examples that I can think of where this has happened.

In Albuquerque, New Mexico, a middle school created a student-run program to help prevent and address the growing bullying problem. The program began after a school-wide survey suggested that there was a quiet, yet serious bullying problem at all grade levels. (According to most teachers, the survey wasn't really necessary; they could tell that morale was low and violent incidents were up.) The problem existed despite the daily, adult-made anti-bullying lessons and videos presented during announcements.

During the initial phase, the student body at each grade level was asked to write the names of three students who they believed were the most trustworthy, approachable, and respected. When I first heard of this selection process, my initial thought was, "How is this not a popularity contest?" My fear was that, without regard to the important traits listed, most students would simply choose the most popular, the most attractive, the most active, the captain of the football team or the cheerleading squad.

I was mistaken.

I had the opportunity to help train the selectees during a retreat, where teachers and counselors guided the student helpers in trust building, listening, and reporting techniques. I found that my initial fear was unfounded, as each and every one of the students proved himself or herself as a truly caring, concerned, and personable candidate. Their peers had known something that I hadn't. These were the students they trusted. And after three months, student surveys showed better morale, better problem solving, and less fear. The culture in the school was noticeably more open and collaborative. I was in awe of what these kids had created and sustained.

Another example comes from Montgomery County Public Schools in Rockville, Maryland. The Board of Education is made up of not only the elected members of the board, but also elected members of the student body from several different schools. The student members attend meetings, vote on board items, and directly engage the superintendent about student issues that come from surveys. If you have not had a chance to see these student board members in action, I invite you to visit the Montgomery County Public Schools website, where Superintendent Josh Starr keeps videos of these meetings.

Another movement that is growing, aptly named Student Voice (www.stuvoice.org), is made of a band of young leaders across the nation who are pressing for more and more inclusion of student opinions and ideas into the national discussion on public education. Using social media and activism, these students are becoming part of the change that they want to see for their own futures and the futures of those that come after.

All of this shows us that we don't need to micromanage or nitpick or lead our students by the hand every step of the way. We need to give them the tools they need, which will guide them through their self-recognized learning paths. We should let them think and use their creativity and voices. We need to get out of the way for a little while and let them be part of the debate. We need to treat them with respect and as equals. I will showcase a more in-depth look at the student voice in chapter 5.

They Need Us to Inspire Them

I heard it from a very passionate, preservice schoolteacher recently: "I love history! I can't wait to share my passion with my students!" This is a great attitude for a new teacher to have when being prepared to enter this challenging profession and it's nice to see teachers model their passion and their own love of learning. I had the same feelings about math and science as a preservice teacher. My eyes were opened to the wonders of the sciences, and I couldn't wait to open my students' eyes, too!

I heard that exact line in early 2005 from one of my classmates in college. She was a history buff who loved reading period literature and, even back then, was blogging about the things she'd learned or loved (did we call it blogging back then?). Her mock lessons were fascinating and eye-opening and her facial expressions while presenting them were almost enough to keep an audience on its toes. Two years after we graduated, I saw her at a district professional development session and almost didn't recognize her.

The smile was gone, the passion was faded, and the excitement of sharing her expertise was wilted to nothing. It became apparent that her dream had not coalesced and, the last I'd heard, she had returned to college to pursue higher education in order to teach at the college level.

The problem was that the passion that she felt and the excitement that her colleagues showed weren't applicable, and certainly less transferable, to the crushing policies of the school district. It's not her fault, but it happens very often. "Why don't they care?" is a pretty common question/complaint from teachers, young and old, new and veteran. The answer is pretty simple: despite the giddiness that adults feel when approached with such knowledge and discovery, we have not given these kids a reason to care. I know that seems harsh and almost insulting to our craft and our love of our subjects, but it's the simple, honest truth. Our students are not automatically tuned in to the pleasure of learning when the end game is a passing score on a test.

My coworker designed beautifully crafted lectures and activities that were loaded with showmanship and excitement. She also created assessments that were perfectly aligned to standards and let her students use the notes from those lectures to answer the mostly-short-answer questions. Finally, she crafted a final project where students were asked to pick the most interesting time period that they had studied, write a report about what might be considered pop culture at the time, and design a period costume. She tried so hard to do everything right, but by the time the state tests rolled around it all meant nothing. That's not what those tests measure.

Another, more modern example comes from a colleague whose students loved his teaching style. He was passionate about science, loved to interact with middle school kids, gave them to freedom to find things out through inquiry and investigation, and used performance assessments to gauge competency and proficiency. It was everyone's favorite class. Then came the arrival of the SMART Board.[2]

It was exciting to get such an awe-inspiring and hyped piece of new century technology installed in their classroom, and even the students were sharing stories about what they'd seen in other rooms and what the possibilities might be. The energy was palpable. Two weeks later, that energy was gone. I have spent some time on this story on my blog, where I discuss the promises and punishments of technology in the classroom. The ending isn't a happy one, however, and ends with the teacher frustrated that his students lost interest in his class so easily. Technology isn't the answer when its use is mandated and it narrows the learning, whether it's a SMART Board or a new class set of computers on which to take Common Core assessments and pretests.

The first section of this chapter, "They Need Us to Understand Them," is the prerequisite to the ability to inspire. Rarely does a new teacher walk into a classroom, just start teaching, and hold the attention and inspire the hard work and dedication from a class of preadolescents for an entire school year. Personally, I've never met one of those mythical educators. (If you are one of them, please contact me.) It takes practice, meaningful reflection and collaboration among colleagues and students to *learn* how to inspire and motivate our kids. And it gets harder every year, with every new mandate that takes away our focus on real, natural learning.

I mentioned that educational leaders need to support these teachers, and by that I mean that there needs to be some *professional development*. More than a few readers cringed at the mention of those two italicized words and that's because professional development seems to have very little to do with student learning and development and everything to do with leading educators to accept the newest, worthless mandate from above. Read on about how the Common Core State Standards Initiative has made the professional development arena completely toxic in today's school systems.

They Need Us to Prepare Them

This section is a little different from the others, for a couple of reasons. The first is that the previous sections are nothing particularly new, but maybe have the need to be *re*newed. This last section, though, is at the heart of what this book is intended for: thinking about our preparation for the unknown and mostly unpredictable movement into the 21st century. The second reason is that our students can tell you that they expect their teachers to perform the other sections as part of their jobs. Most students, however, have no idea what's in store for them in the next five to ten years, so it will be our place—parents and teachers—to make sure they are prepared. And we have to let them take a part in their own learning.

We've heard it over and over again: our current curricula and methods are mirrored closely to those that were created to educate a 19th-century agrarian society; and we have only seen major changes to fit a 20th century industrial society.[3] It's true! Nothing much has changed since then, but we can't say that things flatlined over that time period. There were some times

51

when truly revolutionary practices and designs were put into play and things looked totally different in classrooms. Those revolutionary educators—and those before them—tell us that the climate of standardized testing and the accountability measures that come with it are suffocating the creativity out of students and the innovation of teachers. There are still many teachers who are moving their classes in new directions using their creativity, innovation, and the collaboration with people they work with to create truly effective practices. The problem is that it's getting so difficult, that we *all* aren't doing this and, seriously, we *all* need to be doing this together.

It's very difficult to predict what the world will look like 20, 30, or 100 years from now. We can look backwards at the changes that have happened over the past 20 years and realize that the next 20 will be very different. That means using a 19th century model of teaching would be the most harmful thing that we can collectively do at this point. The old model attempted to move kids from one prescribed level to the next with the necessary skills that were deemed appropriate. The old models tried to rank and file our kids as they progressed through school. Of course, affluence played a big part, as did race.

After a break from this rigid type of teaching in the 1980s and 90s, we have been regressing for the past decade; we call the regressive program of the decade the Common Core State Standards Initiative (CCSSI). The architects of the CCSS tout the standards as being revolutionary in preparing students for the workforce of the future. A few of the CCSS sound deceptively good, using the literacy standards across content areas and the math practices as examples. However, I think we're seeing more of what didn't work previously: one-size-fits-all knowledge and skills standards, building on top of each other, with very little idea of how they are useful in the future lives of our students, other than to classify them as workers and laborers. Even worse, they have opened the floodgates for a slew of new testing regimes and privatization movements. In a climate where student testing has become problematically often and intense, this is the last thing we need to be striving for.

Look at the math standards for K-8: The ultimate goal of reaching calculus in high school is still present, with an emphasis on Algebra I in 8th grade.[4] All of this was pretty important during the middle of the 20th century, since we had to have lots of scientists with solid math and science backgrounds to build rockets, probes, and weapons during the Cold War, using little more than slide rules and program-on-the-fly computers.

It's still important to have scientists; but now, in the 21st century, it's much more important to have a literate society—and more importantly, a *mathematically* and *scientifically* literate society. Therein lays the difference between then and now: The current model seeks to prepare walking libraries of scientific knowledge, facts, vocabulary, and formulas so they can solve quick, shallow problems on the spot using their brains. The new model we need should prepare students to be able to find and

53

understand many different types of information, analyze data, work collaboratively to achieve a desired result, and communicate that result across a global audience.

In the 20th century, we had the luxury of guessing what our students would (or could) be when they grew up. Now, we have no idea (although, as you will see, many entities are investing millions to try to meet the goals that come from corporate gambling). That's because a growing number of jobs that our kids may hold *don't yet exist*.[5] Tell that little snippet to a room of 8th or 9th graders and you will see lots of looks of confusion. What they're thinking is, "then how will I know what to do to get ready?" Tell that snippet to a group of veteran teachers, and you hear almost as many opinions as there are teachers. Unfortunately, there is no real consensus, with one side saying, "More skills, more homework, more practice!" and the other side saying, "More technology, more inquiry, more critical thinking!" There is, of course, a majority in the middle ground saying, "Both, but how?"

Over a dozen states have opted-out from the NCLB requirements as of this writing, and several more have applied to be opted out. But, when you read about the victory of opting out, you also see something else: just because those states are free of NCLB accountability measures, doesn't mean they're all moving in a totally new direction. In fact, the Department of Education is allowing these waivers with the understanding that the states will be able to show the same data using slightly different measures. We are breaking free of NCLB in order to be trapped again by Race to the Top (RttT). Different name; larger, more frightening beast.

Our students need us to help prepare them for their own futures and the future of their country as a continued player in the global economy. The politics at the national and state levels are not going to do it. The boards of education are not going to do it. The president and his education secretary are not going to do it. The for-profit test development companies are certainly not going to do it. This is our job—parents and teachers. We need to speak out and advocate for our kids and prepare them for their real futures. And we must do it together.

To get started, as the introduction to this chapter reminds us, our students need us to remember why we're here in the first place. Then, with all of us working together, we can get education back on track to where we all want and *need* it to be. Their futures depend on it. Consequently, our nation's economic security depends on it. Our first order of business is to get rid of the Common Core State Standards.

Children of the Core

2

A Brief History of Education Reform

"Nothing is more misleading to the youth of a nation than to state the outcome immediately after the beginning as if nothing could have taken place in between."

- Gustav Stresemann

The focus of this book is certainly not the politics behind all of this—there are several very good books on that subject already—but I do have to dig into the history a bit in order to portray a basic idea of how this all came to be. How did the Common Core Network so easily and quickly nationalize and begin to privatize our educational system? Actually, this is nothing new or revolutionary; just like any right-wing, corporate takeover of a public institution, we won't let them just walk in the front door and start changing everything. They had to find a trickier way.

Every successful institution needs a strong foundation. The institution of corporate school reform may look like a silent coup, but it's been well planned for and experimented with for a while now. And it's been up and down. Until now. Now, the institution of corporate education reform has a strong foundation to make its mission complete: the Common Core State Standards.

Academic standards in public schools are not new by any means. National standards, however, are something that many people feared and which took the powers of Federal mandate, in response to a fake crisis, to make happen. Now, conservatives and liberals have a common enemy.[1]

During the Reagan presidency, a false crisis was created in education during an American recession and while observing an economically booming Japan. Our Asian ally was showing us that we were not the only economic power to be reckoned with, and we believed that Japan's rigid educational process was responsible for their stunning growth. At the time, Japan subscribed to a national set of standards and common assessments. We were afraid of losing our spot as the strongest economic power on Earth, and we needed to know how to secure that spot.

It was during this scare that corporate lobbies began to try to convince the public and the government that measured accountability was necessary to give America the educational edge it needed. Our educational system was always considered the envy of the world, but we were told that this honor was slipping through our fingers, and the only way to rescue it was to adopt a private business model, rather than the democratic (yet outdated) system we were used to. We had to find out if our students were going to graduate at the ready to make our country strong. Standardized tests, of course, were considered the only scientifically reliable system to accomplish this, as you'll see in the next few chapters.

Later, during the GOP surge in the House of Representatives during the Clinton presidency, several facets of Federal education control were scrapped, but Clinton was able to hold on to several accountability measures (including standardized tests) in order to measure the progress of Title I initiatives, which served the poorer urban and rural schools with extra funding. During this time, it was noticed that "the achievement gap" was growing, despite the best intentions of child healthcare and educational measures. It was believed that Federal accountability controls needed to be expanded and this set the stage for No Child Left Behind (NCLB).

George W. Bush was all too happy to "reach across the aisle" to enact sweeping education reform to boost school accountability and student progress tracking systems. Testing corporations were all too happy to fill in the need for state assessments, as ordered by the new law. Contrary to a "small government" philosophy, the neoconservative Executive Branch, in one stroke of Bush's pen, nationalized public education. Effectively, if states wanted Title I funds from the Federal government, they were required to show adequate yearly progress (AYP) for *all* students in *all* schools. If they didn't, they could lose that funding, or worse, lose the failing schools.[2]

As recent memory tells us, the initiative was never fully funded, the bar was set impossibly high, and schools found themselves having a very difficult time reaching the adequate yearly progress that the Federal government required. Teachers, who were busy preparing their students for life and college, found themselves under intense pressure to show growth and achievement through standardized test scores. Teachers of English-language learners, special needs students, and other underserved subgroups found themselves feeling like the anchor that slowed the school down. These tests confirmed what the NAEP had told us a decade earlier regarding the "achievement gap" against family income and demographics. Teachers began to speak up, and so did parents.

Partisan politics played a part in feigning concern. The Secretary of Education under President Obama, Arne Duncan, told us all he was listening and started the infamous waiver program. He said he agreed that the "one-size-fits-all" policies under NCLB were failing and that states could show AYP in a different manner than prescribed under the old law. If a state education department could impress Mr. Duncan with an innovative way to account for student achievement, he would graciously allow them to "opt out" of No Child Left Behind. If it sounded too good to be true, that's because it was.

"Superman" had come to town. "He" has had many names since then: Arne Duncan. Michelle Rhee. David Coleman. Joel Klein. ALEC. Sam Walton. Bill Gates. Eli Broad. Yes, even Barack Obama.[3]

Unfortunately, for all of us, this new alternative is much, much worse than NCLB. Race to the Top has started a new, wicked game. Instead of proving progress for funding, the waived states compete for it by drafting educational plans for improvement, which have to follow very strict guidelines. One of those guidelines during round one was the adoption of the Common Core State Standards, which had already been drafted by two groups with strong political and corporate ties by 2009, and which were released in 2010. (The government and corporate groups responsible for starting the movement started the work to nationalize standards as early as 1996.)

So, accountability has taken a new turn. States that have adopted the Common Core and are locked into the testing requirements are accountable to the Federal government. Local school districts, therefore, are required to relinquish their decision-making to the state level. And all states are required to prove proficiency, using scores from a growing battery of tests, to the Federal government. All students, in all schools, from all states must show measurable growth and proficiency, using objective standards and unrealistic benchmarks in order to stay in business. The rules of the "old school" (NCLB) still apply when it comes to failing schools, which include sanctions, up to and including reorganization, closing, or sale to private corporations.[4]

This is why Common Core is so bad for our country. It has put almost all control of public education in the hands of the Federal government, rather than democratically at the local level. The Common Core is the foundation of a larger movement that is profiting from a false crisis in America. The privatizers and testing companies were waiting in the wings for this. The Federal government has set unrealistic goals, the testing companies are providing unrealistic metrics, and the corporations and investors in private charters are waiting to claim their prizes. All of this at the expense of poor, mostly minority students. And the timing was impeccable: all three parts of this movement (Federal government, testing corporations, and privatizers) came together in perfect harmony to take advantage of a constructed crisis.

All of this work, all of this planning, while intentionally ignoring the real cause of failing schools. Unfortunately, President Johnson's "War on Poverty" died long ago. And as we know now (yet continue to debate), poverty has the biggest measurable effect on educational achievement. And even worse, there exists an ongoing effort by the education "reform" movement to debunk the strongly supported hypothesis that affluence, or lack thereof, is the best indicator of academic performance.

I constantly attack the Common Core State Standards Initiative because it is the foundation of the institution responsible for hurting our schools, our teachers, and our kids. And it's not an accident. The Common Core State Standards were built with one main goal in mind: to standardized learning in preparation for standardized testing so that testing companies could sell billion-dollar contracts with state education departments. Why? Under Race to the Top, the states are required to purchase those contracts with Race to the Top funds (which almost never cover the costs). It's a vicious cycle and the states (all but 5) are trapped. [California is not trapped, yet, but is being carved up by a new way to allow individuals districts to waive their NCLB testing mandates in exchange for RttT mandates (Race to the Top, Round 3)]. This won't stop until public education in America is nationalized, deemed to fail, and sold to private corporations and charter management companies.

Every strong institution needs a reliable foundation. The strong institution of corporate education reform has a strong foundation that has tricked state education departments into believing this is best for our kids. That foundation is called the Common Core State Standards Initiative. Without it, the corporations responsible for rapidly dismantling our democratic system of education would have nothing on which to build.

Children of the Core

3

This is How Democracy Ends

"Democracy cannot succeed unless those who express their choice are prepared to choose wisely. The real safeguard of democracy, therefore, is education."

- Franklin Delano Roosevelt

Almost a year ago, I offered my time to the middle school at which I was employed to give a two-night presentation that promised to ease parents' concerns about the Common Core State Standards (CCSS) and the tightly-aligned Connected Mathematics Program (CMP). My boss, my coworkers, and many of those parents gave me kudos. We talked about the future, the upcoming tests by the Smarter Balanced Assessment Consortium (SBAC), and we even did some hands-on math demonstrations. It was a good time for me and I hope those parents can say the same.

My message was simple: *trust us—we've got this!* Some of my audience members were still skeptical, and they should be praised for that skepticism.

First, I want to offer you my apologies. It wasn't long after my presentation that I had a crushing realization that the entire thing (minus the hands-on stuff) was completely misguided. I felt like a flip-flopper, but I've always valued the truth more than feeling good about myself. So, I had to clear the air. The truth hurts and it should start scaring the hell out of you, because your children are your most precious gift and you will do anything to protect them.

The whole reason I was part of the team that put those presentations together was to ease your worry about the changes that were coming. I'm here to retract everything I said. You should be worried. *Very* worried! I was wrong. The Common Core State Standards is a sham, the Smarter Balanced Assessment Consortium is an instrument of devastation, and it's all run by the "Common Core Network" you see in the following Venn diagram (don't you love Venn diagrams?):

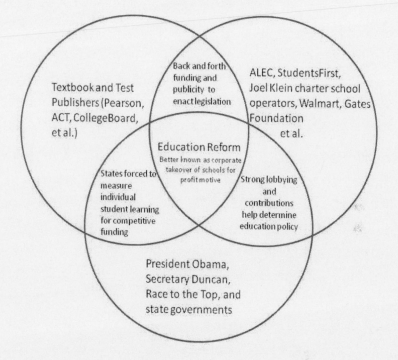

Before this starts sounding too nutty, let me get down to the reality. You'll see that I'm not exaggerating.

America has long been known—despite our problems—as the country of freedom, innovation, and wealth. There are several reasons for this, not the least of which is our democratic and free public education system. Prior to NCLB in 2002, and Race to the Top eight years later, standardization was limited to SAT and ACT tests, NAEP and PISA tests, and graduation exams for Advanced Placement courses. We valued music, art, drama, languages and the humanities just as much as we valued science, math, and English (for the most part). We believed in a well-rounded education.

Now, the Common Core State Standards has one goal: to create common people. The accompanying standardized tests have one purpose: to enforce standardized learning. Why? Because the movers and the shakers have a vested interest in it. It's about money and it's about making sure all that money stays in one place.[1]

It's been happening for many years already. StudentsFirst, ALEC, the Walton and Broad and Gates Foundations, and other lobbying groups have created and supported a false crisis in American education. They want you to believe that America is in sad educational shape so that they can play the heroes: when the standardized tests show that our public schools can't meet the demands of the CCSS, private charter operators will swoop down and save your kids.[2]

However, what they've begun is a snowball effect of legislation that devastates public education, teacher careers, student engagement and fulfillment, and an already underfunded school system so that they can replace the public system, the unions, and the government employees with private systems that promise to pay less, bust unions, and remove benefits and pensions.

Public funds for education are increasingly up for grabs by private corporations (including so-called nonprofits) and are being funneled away from public schools. School closures are epidemic in urban areas and teachers are being let go, forced into early retirement, or they leave due to poor conditions and treatment.

Teach For America, which puts college graduates through a crash course in teaching to the test, is a prime example of an institution that steals government funding, places it in the hands of private corporations, and effectively removes that pesky career (tenure) teacher problem. It's worked like a dream: the average TFA teacher stays in the classroom for about 2-3 years, and only a few remain for 5 or more years. So, the new American teacher is a mass-produced, temporary worker in an ongoing assembly line. Is it really cheaper? Not usually. And TFA teachers don't complain about pay, pensions, or benefits, since this is often just a step in their career ladders.

But, this also means that students don't have highly-qualified and seasoned teachers leading their learning anymore. Even worse that that, TFA teachers are prepared and trained with test data as the be-all-to-end-all of priorities. These teachers only know effectiveness by the scores their students receive on standardized tests.[3]

What about cooperation? Collaboration? Creativity? Communication? Critical thinking? Life skills? Those skills only make it into the curriculum if there's time (which there isn't) and you can't expect it to be integrated or cohesive. That's not what the training is for. Our students are now part of a larger plan: to prepare them for the "college and career readiness" laid out by the "job creators" on Wall Street—the ones that want your kids to understand that a job is what they're trained for and they are lucky to have, so stop whining about your pensions and benefits. And forget about belonging to one of those pesky unions—we will have outlawed them completely by then.

More importantly, all of the skills listed above lead our students to be profound, critical, and meaningful participants in a modern democracy. Some would argue that our days as a free country for the people and by the people are limited, and running out fast. If we continue to support the path that our nation's educational system is on, we will speed up the end of our democracy. When students are forced to learn for the sake of a score and are denied the opportunity to think and reason and question and appreciate the world in which they live, they are all the more easy to control and deny basic rights.

America did not become what it is today because of common people who have common backgrounds with common education and common thoughts. We didn't get where we are today because of convergent thinking. We got here, with our innovations and achievements, because of *divergent* thinking.

We celebrate our diversity, exceptionality, and bravery at the same time that we are attempting to bury those traits. The world is following our educational models of the past few decades at the same time that we are turning our backs on those successful models. We are digging a grave for our democratic process at a time when we should be paying extra special attention to keeping it healthy.

Our next generation of learners can save us and keep us strong (if we let them) through their diversity, ingenuity, creativity, friendliness, cooperation, and forward thinking. And their dreams. The Common Core State Standards, standardized tests, and privatized teacher corps are stifling those dreams. Our democracy will ultimately be the victim.

A Reality Check

Let's look for a moment at a majority (yet shrinking) consensus among professional educators and the perspective that the public has been fed regarding the Common Core State Standards. This is part of a comment left by a professional educator on my blog:

> *I have a hard time believing that the whole thing is a ploy to destroy education and teachers. I doubt that our country would maliciously hurt our children.*

I include this comment because it's a good start to a list of things that teachers and parents have been told to believe and talk about (read: memorize and recite). We are supposed to trust our educational and government leaders. They would never hurt our kids or allow our kids to be hurt. First, let's talk about what

71

the Common Core State Standards Initiative is and what it isn't. Then, I'll come back to discuss our trust in our country.

Following is a non-inclusive list of myths about the Common Core State Standards and standardized testing, which professional teachers have all been ordered to accept. I will touch on why each one is not a truth or a benefit to our kids or to the future of our country.[4]

Myth: Common Core is *not* a step toward national standards.

Reality: Whether the standards were designed to nationalize education is debatable. The official FAQ of the CCSSI sounds a little defensive in answering the question of nationalized education. They explain that the standards aren't national because the Federal government wasn't the entity that drafted them. I am arguing that the CCSS *are* national standards, meant to standardize education across the country and prescribe what business interests want to see in the next generation of workers.

The fact that 45 states and 3 territories (plus the DoD education system) have adopted the standards points to a pretty strong buy-in. CCSSI suggests that the choice to create, adopt, and implement the standards was state-led. Even if the initiative was not born with nationalization in mind, that's what it's evolved into—and it takes a serious shortage of foresight or critical thinking to believe that such a project could have any other purpose. The CCSSI was created for one purpose: to standardize the way our kids are educated to prepare them for a future that has already been designed for them.

Obama's Education Department has assured state buy-in by tying funds to the adoption of the CCSS; at the same time state budgets have cut education funds to near nothing, thereby invalidating the idea that this is a state-led initiative. In other words, there is hardly any real choice in the matter. Adopt the Core, or starve.

Myth: Teachers helped create the Common Core State Standards.

Reality: Almost every page of the CCSSI website includes a passage that makes sure everyone know that teachers, administrators, and educational experts were in on the development of the standards. However, there is no real evidence for this claim. Which teachers? From where? Are there credits to these contributing teachers or their schools? (The contributors acknowledged by the CCSSI include three teachers and a handful of cheerleaders for the CCSS or people like me, who have changed their minds after it was too late.) Perhaps the NEA and AFT—the largest teacher unions in the country—supported and gave feedback to the initiative, but they were not instrumental in constructing the standards.

In fact, the Council of Chief State School Officers (CCSSO) and the National Governors Association (NGA) were the true contributors and signers of the initiative, and both groups have debatable abilities to lead educational reform. The face of the CCSSI, David Coleman, is a businessman, lawyer, and lobbyist, with ties to testing and textbook corporations. He is now the CEO of College Board–the high-power testing corporation that brings us the SAT, AP exams, and lots of professional development (which is only geared toward College Board products). Mr. Coleman has been a loud voice, among many, that propagandizes a false "crisis in America," joining the likes of Michelle Rhee and her network of deceptive education reformers. Do you see a relationship developing here that's just a *little* too comfortable–and profitable?

Myth: The Common Core State Standards are evidence-based.

Reality: That statement is very vague, and ironically, there is no evidence that the CCSS are evidence-based. The evidence that is cited so often by Common Core proponents includes U.S. and international benchmarks and how those benchmarks led to achievement on standardized tests, including NAEP, PISA, TIMSS, and others. Saying that other standards are the evidence that these standards are effective doesn't makes logical sense. The CCSS were built just right so that standardized tests would be the best way to evaluate the effectiveness of teachers, textbooks, and curricula. They do not provide a system or a goal for student success (and the CCSSI doesn't seem to clearly claim that they do). They have never been tested or used before, and public education groups have very lightly evaluated them. As more and more study is done on the CCSS, the more it's becoming clear that the standards were written in spite of the evidence, especially in reading.

If anything, there has been more evidence against the need or efficacy of the Common Core. The more they are analyzed and reflected upon, the more damaging they seem to be. Although supporters will often point to the countries that we modeled the Core after (South Korea, Japan, etc.), we must also remember that these countries have abandoned those models, since they have been shown to damper innovation and growth. It's interesting that the U.S. has adopted overturned Asian models of education at the same time that those same Asian countries have begun to implement the more open, democratic, and progressive American model that we have thrown in the trash. Perhaps the skill and drill methods did help Asian economies get to where they are, but many recognize that to move their economies into the 21st century, they need to change things up. We have chosen, in effect, to go backwards.

Myth: The Common Core standards increase rigor.

Reality: The slogan that has gained traction and faithfulness is "fewer, clearer, higher." This may be true for some states, but not all. High school standards, in particular, are numerous, vague, and not generally cohesive. It's anyone's guess what the "higher" means in that slogan, but I'll assume that it means more students passing achievement tests (it certainly doesn't refer to higher-order thinking). Some experts might define rigor as meaning "harder." If this is the functional definition, then yes, they are more rigorous.

That's only because, compared to other state standards, skills and concepts have been pushed to earlier grade levels, which has already caused its own set of headaches for students and teachers. This has been a major point of contention, since it's been shown that the CCSSI set objectives that are unrealistic and way beyond reading and math levels for certain age groups. Here's an example from a third-grade assignment, aligned well to the Common Core:

> *Mount Everest is considered the highest mountain— above sea level—in the world, but it's not really the tallest. Measured from its base on the floor of the ocean, Mauna Kea, in Hawaii, is 33,476 feet tall. Only the top 13,796 of Mauna Kea are above sea level.*

The reading alone is more than challenging for most third graders, but look at the question prompt that came with it:

> *Mount Everest is the highest mountain, but Mauna Kea is the tallest mountain. Write the reason that the tallest and the highest mountain are not the same. Provide evidence to support your answer.*[5]

I wish I was exaggerating when I say that several parents have reported their kids becoming very anxious about this assignment, even to the point of crying and wanting to stay home the next day. This isn't "rigor;" this is abuse.

I, and several other teachers and professors, define rigor as using background and new knowledge to solve novel problems using creativity and collaboration. Rigor should be defined in terms of the methods used to learn, not the difficulty our instruction or the amount of work students are given. The CCSS does not increase rigor as it should be defined in the new century; it decreases it and effectively "dumbs down" the overall curriculum.

Myth: The Common Core will help our kids be "college and career-ready."

Reality: This is the myth that deserves the most incredulity. Going back to the fact that the most prominent forces behind the CCSSI are testing corporations, state chiefs, and governors, who do you think came up with this one? The only evidence that these standards lead students to be college and career-ready are the promises of College Board, and ACT—the same folks that decide whether or not you get into college using one big, expensive, and stressful test each. Now, go back to the introduction of this book and look at the five most important applied skills for success after high school. None of those skills are included in the CCSS. And schools don't have time to develop those applied skills due to the immense amount of time and money being spent on low-level skills prescribed by the CCSS.

Incidentally, it's worth noting that the CCSSI defends its ability to prepare kids for college and career in one sentence, and in another sentence, blatantly denies its ability to help fix education. Passing the buck is a specialty with these people.

Let's pretend for a moment that it was okay to let the CCSS lead our kids to be "college and career ready," and that the tests themselves were valid and showed how well each child was advancing toward the goal of getting into college or entering the workforce prepared. What are we missing? Keep in mind that the CCSS, the accompanying tests, and the policies that wrap around it all are focused on student achievement in math and English/language arts. I think that word, *achievement*, is a key word here, and it is a bad word. Achievement signifies that there is a single goal in mind, and that students who reach that goal have achieved. "Growth" is another feel-good word, used by Obama's Department of Education, which is a poor use of terms. Again, growth simply suggests students' or schools' advancement toward a single achievement objective. We have then narrowed our curriculum and teaching in order to reach just one or two main objectives—namely high or growing test scores against the Common Core State Standards.

Later, I will discuss how test scores don't show that students are prepared for college or career (and how some higher education institutions are beginning to recognize this). Right now, it's important to know that being proficient and achieving high scores against content standards absolutely does not prepare our kids for college or career. This system—the Common Core Network—only prepares kids to grow into compliant, no-questions-asked, nose-to-the-grindstone, low-wage workers in an assembly line of trained and traded employees. Again, I wish I could say I was exaggerating.

Myth: The Common Core focuses not just on *what* kids learn, but *how* they learn.

Reality: This doesn't make any sense, because there is not a shred of evidence to support it. The CCSS are just what they say they are: academic standards. Nowhere in the documents can you find any suggestion of a focus on how kids learn. This was a major point of frustration for hundreds of schoolteachers who found themselves needing to get ready for Common Core. It was also a major profit machine for textbook and test publishers who were just waiting to offer the "professional development" and material support that everyone so desperately needed.

The claim that the CCSSI focuses on how kids learn comes from one idea: the learning and topic strands in the standards build on top of each other as the years pass. This is not a change in focus, since this is simply copying what teachers have known for centuries, if not millennia. To suggest that the CCSS are focusing on how kids learn, without any evidence, is to purvey an outright lie.

Several people (teachers, administrators, legislators, parents, and even students) have told me that it doesn't make sense to attack the Common Core since they're just standards. I disagree. They are not "just standards." They are an untested, overrated, and dangerous attempt to standardize our workforce training programs (formerly known as public schools) and track students into pre-qualified ranks and positions in the American economic class structure.

This fits nicely with the ongoing attacks that StudentsFirst, Teach For America, Bill and Melinda Gates, The Broad Foundation, the Walton family, and Democrats for Education Reform have sustained. As Kentucky schools showed recently, the mix of new standardized tests and the Common Core State Standards leads to dismal drops in school scores.[6] How many more schools, districts, and states will see the same problems? How long will it take for teachers and schools to be the ultimate scapegoats of those failures? How long will it take for bad policy to remove good teachers and replace them with mass-produced teachers with 6 weeks of training in test administration and little else?

How long will it take to derail public education in this country and replace it with a model that serves the wealthy power elite, which really has no interest in making sure your child can think critically, creatively, or independently? As David C. Berliner, visiting professor at the Columbia University Teachers College, suggests, "The driving force for business' interest in education is the productivity of the American workforce."[7]

There is no investment being made in our children that helps them grow as citizens in a modern democratic society. The only investments being made now are dedicated to making them useful, compliant, and obedient workers.

So, is this a "ploy to destroy education and teachers," as stated in the comment? If we're talking about our ideal, free, democratic, and well-rounded system, then yes. It is most clearly a plan to change our system into a private, profit-driven model.

Are the country's educational architects "maliciously" trying to hurt our children? No. I don't think they are targeting children with the hopes of destroying their lives. However, I do believe they are looking at the most efficient ways to fill low-level workforces in the near future. In other words, they aren't trying to hurt your kids; they simply don't care about any of them as living, breathing human beings. To the business elite, the testing corporations, the government, and the privatizers, our children are simply numbers. Those numbers are based on test scores that will help guide them into the fields that will help the corporate world maximize profits the most.

The Common Core State Standards were designed to keep us all on the same page, learning the same things, and being taught the same, corporate-prescribed skills (which do not focus on liberal thinking and reasoning). It's so much easier to track and place an entire country's workforce that way.

The Threat to American Kids

A lot of people who haven't spent a lot of time with the CCSS have asked me, "How can a set of standards ruin our democracy?" or "Don't you think that it's a good thing to have everyone on the same page?" My first answer is an invitation to read the standards, see how they change by grade level, try to match them to the cognitive levels of their respective age groups, and see if you think anything's missing. Finally, ask yourself if you think that *every* high school graduate could or *should* have all of these standards mastered by the end of 12th grade.

Once you have looked over the Common Core State Standards for yourself, then I invite you to read the strong opposition I have collected here. This is not deeper thinking, clearer organization, better rigor, higher expectations, or a stronger nation. This is how we widen the achievement gap and the nation's divisions by socioeconomic status and income and wealth distribution. The Common Core State Standards Initiative is the latest craze in response the latest fake national crisis and a huge distraction from the real problems affecting our students, those problems that are smoldering beneath the surface—out of sight and out of mind.

Most dangerously, our public education is being simultaneously assaulted by the three entities in the Common Core Network. It's difficult to see the big picture if we are most focused on one at a time. We may be worried about aligning our curricula to the Common Core standards while our lawmakers are being paid to pass legislation requiring more testing by Pearson. Or, we may be fighting the increased standardized testing structures while state governments pass new laws making closing and replacing schools easier. We are going to have to remain fiercely vigilant.

Children of the Core

4

The Dangers of Standardized Testing

"Nobody grew taller by being measured."

- Roland Meighan

In 1971, Alice Rivlin published a book titled, *Systematic Thinking for Social Action,* which birthed the widespread ideology that all educational outcomes could be measured statistically and scientifically. Included was the idea that what goes in correlates strongly with what comes out. In other words, Avlin believed that student test scores accurately reflected the effectiveness of the learning structures that were delivering instruction.

The following line from Rivlin's book explains why we are still dealing with a growing standardized testing movement today:

"We want the biggest bang for our buck."[1]

It's easy to see why this caught on. In business, the foundational structures strive to be as efficient and as inexpensive as possible, while leading to a maximized outcome. This was a boost to the movement to create a corporate model of education. Teachers must be highly trained, modestly paid, and instruction time must be maximized in order to justify the American education budget. In turn, the outcomes should be reflective of that model, in the business sense. We should have high graduation rates, proficient students at the top the world, and a consistent population of high school graduates ready to enter the workforce. The corporate model also sought an objective and relatively automatic form of accountability. Thus, the NAEP test was perfect: it worked like a business spreadsheet, which would keep track of student performance based on a sample of students in three grade levels.

Testing in schools, up until the 1990s, generally consisted of surveys and polls, which were designed to give educational and government leaders an idea of how students, parents, and teachers felt things were going. Classroom grades were taken into account and survey results were analyzed to inform local policy. The Federal dollars to fund school programs were passed down to districts and schools, where resources could be best allocated to the needs of students and teachers. Basically, schools and teachers were trusted to educate their own students, using the best practices for each district's population.

The National Assessment

In 1994, the first National Assessment of Educational Progress (NAEP) results were published, which included data from around 1970 to 1994 in math, science, and reading for ages 9, 13, and 17. The most obvious trend in the data was the dismal "achievement gap," where African-American and Hispanic-American kids were performing way below their white peers. NAEP continues to publish reports for annual tests in the same subjects every year, and that gap has been persistent. Although scale scores improve every year (with few exceptions), the gap seems to be getting wider.

Unfortunately, the 1994 report card did not include income-based subgroups, so the only measures to correlate proficiency against were location, Title I participation (which is based mostly on income) and race. It's not surprising to us that those kids who lived in inner cities, were from minority subgroups, and participated in Title I programs received the lowest scores—it's something we could have predicted long ago. As a frightening example, consider 12th grade reading proficiency in 1994, where 98% of students proficient were not participating in Title I, yet only 2% of students proficient *were* participating in Title I programs.

The NAEP report makes it clear in its disclosure sections that this should not be an indication of the success or failure of the

Title I program, since outside factors may be at work. And there are many such factors, which are systematically ignored by our policymakers. I will discuss this more as we go along.

What the 1994 NAEP report did accomplish was an awakening, of sorts, where regions and individual states saw a large-scale comparison among themselves. California, as an example, noticed that their kids' scores were some of the lowest in the nation. Also, among the four regions of the U.S. (Northeast, Northwest, Southwest, and Southeast), the Southeast region carried the lowest proficiency rates in all three subjects.[2] It was high time we started making the states accountable for their performance.

State Assessments

In 1994, after the NAEP reports were published, President Bill Clinton signed the Improving America's Schools Act, which allocated additional funding to schools serving low-income and disadvantaged students. States who received these funds were required to create standards and standardized testing systems to account for the effects of increased funding for those schools.

California began using the Standardized Testing and Reporting (S.T.A.R.) system the following year, making test administration from grades 3 - 8 a state law. North Carolina was working on statewide tests the year previous to the report and implemented them shortly thereafter. The purpose for these tests was to find shortfalls in the progress of students and to direct action and funds to those schools. Unfortunately, four years later, despite some growth, the achievement gap grew even wider.

President George W. Bush ran on an education platform that promised an overhaul of America's schools, using statistical measurement as a silver bullet, much like what Alice Rivlin prescribed 30 years earlier. If states wanted funding, they needed to beef up their academic standards and show that all students are growing in proficiency—every year. Schools that didn't show progress could face sanctions, up to and including student school choice (which diverted funding from the original school), state management of the school or district, or even school closings.[3]

NCLB promised those sanctions for failing schools and rewards for schools that met the goal of 100% by the year 2014. Of course, the bar was set so high and with so little time that no school system will ever meet that goal. Every state has a yearly test to meet the NCLB requirements, and every state that has applied for and accepted Race to the Top (RttT) funding has assessments to account for student learning, as well. The biggest difference between NCLB and RttT is this:

NCLB seeks to measure if students are learning.

RttT seeks to measure if teachers are teaching.

Neither can happen using standardized tests, yet both the Bush and Obama administrations endorse and require the use of high-stakes, one-size-fits-all, expensive and highly questionable testing materials to advise education policy, funding, and the futures of thousands of schools and millions of students. The Common Core State Standards, contrary to the rhetoric, emphasize rote memorization, test preparation, and low-level thinking. And that's just beginning. Here are some reasons that standardized testing, as it's being used in this country to measure success against the CCSS, is so very dangerous.

Danger One: Standardized Testing is "Junk Science"

As any 4th grade "little scientist" should be able to tell you, good science starts with a question. NCLB started with George W. Bush's famously ironic question, "Is our children learning?" That 4th grader will then tell you that we need a hypothesis, an answer to that question. It was obvious at the time that the American government answered negatively to Bush's question, even though it was obviously loaded. The problem is that the evidence that brought NCLB to the table wasn't valid. Even worse, the evidence being used to track the success of NCLB is anything but valid.

NCLB was born out of the previous results of the NAEP tests, which showed a broad and widening achievement gap. This was certainly a cause for concern, since there was obviously a trend of inequity among different subgroups, mostly those associated with race, but also between participants and non-participants in

Title I programs. The Bush Administration (and many others) carefully avoided discussing the causation between poverty and test scores, and simply suggested that Title I dollars are not being allocated wisely in the states and districts. It was time for some accountability. And some more bad science.

In a *Time Magazine* op-ed from October 2012, Noliwe Rooks describes the fact that standardized tests are lousy measures of student learning. First of all, variables affecting student learning and testing are not effectively isolated. In other words, testing all kids about the same things, without isolating the content from every other variable invalidates the tests. The two big variables, according to Rooks, are race and socioeconomic status, which it has been shown are heavily biased against in common tests.[4]

Additionally, Dr W. James Popham, who was an Emeritus Professor at UCLA, warned against the effectiveness of NCLB in 1999. He suggested that, as a norm-referenced assessment technique that gauges a students understanding of a topic or concept, these standardized tests do exactly what they're supposed to do. Dr. Popham even praises the good tests for doing that one job extremely well. However, Dr. Popham also advises against using these tests for any other purposes, especially those that try to advise public policy or effectiveness of the teaching and learning system. There are simply too many confounding variables to allow standardized tests to hold any valid measures of causation.

He even offered some advice for parents and teachers who find themselves or their schools being evaluated by such tests:

1 Learn the ins and outs of standardized tests. What they measure, what they cover, why they're administered, who sees the results, and what is done with the students' information.

2 Once you have educated yourself properly, begin a campaign to educate other teachers, parents, policymakers, and community members truly understand what these tests are being used for.

3 Find new ways of better assessing student learning and teacher effectiveness, and then encourage everyone you know to stop participating in the standardized testing regime.[5]

Even before NCLB and RttT required standardized tests as the measures of school effectiveness, the specialists and the scientists knew it couldn't work and were already encouraging people to opt out. Of course, any 4th grade scientist could have told us that too, since most 4th grade scientists know that variables must be isolated in order to show a relationship. Even professional mathematicians and statisticians have come out against the efficacy of these tests.

So, it begs the question: Why did we all seem to be okay with NCLB if our experts knew it was bad? And why are so many people allowing our kids' education to fall into the hands of bad legislation and greedy privatizers?

Danger Two: The Experts Aren't Making Policy

One of the popular social media memes circulating the Internet makes a poignant statement about how teachers and parents feel about our current educational policy: "Those who can, teach; those who can't, make laws about teaching." Another one shows a teacher standing by a blank whiteboard, explaining that it portrays the sum total of educational background of most legislators currently making educational policies. These are posted to break a smile, a snicker, and some head shaking.

Teachers know they are being forced to do things that have nothing to do with teaching or learning. It wasn't always this bad. Teachers and administrators seemed to have a foot in the door of education legislation for a long time, and when our place was threatened, we bargained collectively with districts and school boards. The whole idea behind teacher unions is to put in place practices and laws that make sense for educating kids.

At the same time, a massive and collective movement to take public education away from the public is on the rise. The Great Recession of the new millennium had great timing for the corporate reform movement: it became very easy to point to the excesses of public education budgets and the results that were coming from that investment. (Again, these are business people who are only interested in cold, hard return-on-investment numbers.) Based on the bad science mentioned previously, reformers attacked teachers for being lazy, overpaid, underqualified, and even criminally spoiled by their unions. It goes without saying that there was never any evidence of these ridiculous charges and that there was obviously an ulterior motive behind them.

The attacks on teachers and their pensions and their low scores for underprivileged kids led to a very fast and very clean takeover of educational policymaking. The reform movement discredited teachers' ability to lead and be trusted. Then, when teachers and teacher groups spoke up to defend the schools and the kids, the reformers dismissed them as whiners and even as unpatriotic.

The Common Core State Standards Initiative is the glue that keeps this orchestrated attack together. Thanks to the standards, the government, the corporate charter managers, and the publishing companies can continue with their collective agenda to create and maintain policymaking that is favorable to them. When teachers, universities, experts, or even parents speak up, the corporate reform propaganda machine kicks into high gear to bury, downplay, or divert any dissident action.

When teachers aren't allowed to decide what's best for the students who spend eight hours per day in their classrooms, and when teacher groups can't decide collaboratively what the best practices for their children should be, then we have given our kids' futures to the corporate model that ranks and files them and places them into a constructed future before they can even graduate high school.

The Common Core State Standards are the foundation of that system. All Federal education policy is build from those standards. All student testing and tracking is done against those standards. And now, standardized testing is the focus and the law of all public school curricula, from Kindergarten through 12th grade. This is going to limit and level-down classroom learning in public schools at the moment we most need it to be more open and limitless. In many cases, it already has been severely damaged.

Danger Three: Teachers Can't Use These Expensive Tests

End-of-year, summative exams that students must take in compliance with NCLB are completely useless to teachers and students. Tight security and threat of prosecution and job loss due to any breach keeps the test content completely private. During the test, teachers are not allowed to see what's on the tests. And afterwards, when it's all finished, teachers still can't see what's on the test until months to a year later, when the publishers and government officially release the used items. They're useless because they don't tell us anything that we can use to evaluate our programs, our teaching, our students, or our use of resources. That's because we're not allowed to see them.

We can't match our students' answers to the questions to find misunderstandings, discrepancies, or bad test items. We aren't allowed to see the test items to determine bias or language barriers until our students have left. We just have to trust that the Educational Testing Service, Pearson, and their kin know how to do this and have our kids' best interest at heart. As you have figured out by now, I have a problem with that.

I think the policymakers figured that a lot of us had a problem with that, so they came up with a new system to complement the summative requirements of NCLB. Race to the Top puts this into motion: a testing regime that's aligned with the Common Core State Standards and ranks students against their peers regarding how well they were performing on the standards.

Here's one of the most beautiful points of pro-testing propaganda that is constantly regurgitated by Pearson, McGraw-Hill, and Arne Duncan: *Standardized tests are a tool for teachers to determine how well their students are performing in class and how well they master concepts.* Well, as I mentioned, summative standardized tests are worthless in that regard.

The type of test to which they are referring is called a "formative assessment." It's a tool in every teacher's kit, and good formative assessments are very valuable. They can be as simple as an observation, a single question, a short quiz, a dialogue, a debate, a conference, an essay, or any number of materials. Teachers use informal and formal methods of assessing their students every day, and sometimes more often than that.

So, the testing corporations saw another way to make money: create those formative assessments for school districts, grade them, and send back score reports so that teachers can use the data to inform their instruction. It sounds magnificent. There are two, huge flaws with this system.

First, the tests (also called benchmarks, because they try to measure if every student is where he or she should be, in relation to the rest of the grade level) are based on Common Core, which means that students are being testing against only academic standards, instead of skill and ability standards. This is very limiting to a good education, especially to a good teacher who laments the waste of time, resources, and money to make these tests happen. Second, teacher evaluations are now based, at least in large part, on the scores from these benchmarks.

Danger Four: Test Results Are Used Inappropriately

The educational reform tool du jour is the highly-controversial "value-added measure" of teacher effectiveness, which means that scores from student benchmark or end-of-year tests are factored into teacher evaluations. Since standardized tests are scientifically invalid (as we saw in *Danger One*), you can see how adding value to them as an evaluation tool is also invalid. And unethical.

Take the case of Kim Cook, a first-grade teacher in Florida, a state that currently uses student test scores from benchmarks to count as 40 percent of a teacher's total evaluation score. The rest of the evaluation consists of a lesson study and a principal evaluation. Teachers are given a composite score, based on the three measures of performance and then fit into a category of effectiveness, such as highly effective or unsatisfactory. Mrs. Cook made public the breakdown of her evaluation, with a commentary:

> *My final appraisal for the 2011-2012 school year:*
> > *Evaluation summary scores:*
> > > *Lesson Study: 100/100 points x .20 (20%) = 20 points*
> > > *Principal Appraisal: 88/100 points x .40 (40%) = 35.2 points*
> > > *VAM Data: 10/100 x .40 (40%) = 4 points*
> > *Total points = 59.2 (Unsatisfactory)*
> *The VAM data comes from Alachua Elementary School's FCAT scores; children I NEVER taught, although my opinion wouldn't be different even if I had.*

Her lessons were perfect, according to this model. Her principal gave her a strong appraisal. Her students' test scores showed, as a lone measure, that she has failed. These scores came from a feeder school, for kids that she never taught. The system is obviously (almost comically) broken in this case, but the point is clear: you cannot hold teachers accountable for faulty, unrealistic goals, which are based on shoddy science.

Here's the kicker: Mrs. Cook was named Teacher of the Year that same school year. Her colleagues all agreed that she deserved the highest honor in the school. I would argue that her kids' low test scores can also be a badge of honor—she is more focused on being a great teacher than a test preparation associate.

The worst part of this scenario comes from policies being considered or enacted everywhere. Kim Cook's performance, based on those scores, may soon determine how much she gets paid, whether or not she needs "corrective action," or if she even gets to continue being a teacher. It's happening all over the place.

As Ms. Cook's story reflects, Bill Gates and Pearson both like to say that standardized testing should be accompanied by surveys and principal evaluation. Overall, those latter measures have been consistently high for effective teachers, where standardized test scores serve only as outliers, which directly contradict true measures of good teaching.

In North Carolina, as in many other states, the Department of Public Instruction has left the use and interpretation of end-of-course tests up to the districts. After the NCLB- and RttT-required reporting has been taken care of, the districts may use them for whatever they please. Unfortunately, the districts have all seemed to agree that attaching these summative evaluations to final course grades is a good idea, copying an antiquated college model.

Some districts call for the tests to account for 20%, with some as high as 30% of the total, final grade. When there are so many better ways to assess a student's understanding of course content and performance, it doesn't make sense to base a student's grade on junk science.

Danger Five: Kids Learn that Life is a Multiple-Choice Test

I recently had a driven discussion with my daughter about her high school classes (she would replace the word "driven" with "frustrating"). Her assignment was to take the role of president for a day and give relatively quick solutions to complex issues and problems facing our country today–with some exaggerations. The discussion started when she asked me about money, the economy, the best educational system in the world, and some other opinions.

She then took out the paper on which the assignment was printed and read off no fewer than 8 very complex issues that she was being asked to solve, more or less, in about 2 hours.

I asked when it was due. She said tomorrow.

My eyes widened.

Hers rolled.

My daughter is an overachiever. Her understanding of the assignment was to research as much as possible about each of those issues and what has been done so far to tackle them, and then write a well-studied and correct paper. In other words, she was looking the *right answer*. I told her that I don't think that was what her teacher had in mind. If he gave one night to complete this assignment, then I was sure he was asking for ideas based on background knowledge, not a full analysis, followed by drafts of legislation. My daughter, being a teenager, argued with me for a little while (about 45 minutes), and then came to agree with me.

Her problem? She doesn't "work that way." I know she doesn't. Neither have many of the students I've taught over the years. Why? Because they are trained to either know or find the *right answer*. This is a little frustrating for me, because in the 21st century world, there often isn't a *right answer*.

I muttered that she wouldn't have this problem if high schools ran under my rules. She had to ask, so I told her.

The culture of standardized testing requires correct answers. In mathematics, that's fine (although there is always room for creativity there, too), but in every other core subject, training students to seek "correct answers" is not only boring and stifling to student creativity, it's also dangerous.

Every time Arne Duncan touts his Race to the Top grants as a way to boost innovation, I feel a little nauseated. There is no way that preparing students for standardized tests, pigeonholing students by ability, and focusing on the Common Core at the expense of arts, humanities, and sports is boosting innovation. Duncan's program is crushing that innovation under the weight of one-size-fits-all curriculum and single-minded progress metrics.

If her high school courses ran the way I would want to see, the assignment would start with a complex question, which had a complex answer. No, *several* complex answers. That's the way the world works. (You can't ask high school students to solve the healthcare issues in this country by finding the *right answer*, but most of them will try to anyway, and will want to know if they got it.) Those several complex answers would be the basis for discussion and debate. Then, further research. Then, more discussion and debate. Then, a final proposal and presentation and maybe even a blog post, which is all way more revealing about student learning than a multiple-choice test.

I strongly believe that one of the reasons that high school students either drop out or aren't "career and college ready" is because they are so worried about finding the *right answers*. And when they don't get the right answer after a certain number of tries? Screw it; I quit.

I also strongly believe that standardized testing and the culture of being right all the time (the American way!) needs to change if we plan to stay competitive in this global knowledge economy. There's just too much information; there are too many potentially "right" answers. We don't need to learn how to find the *right answer;* we need to learn how to find *new* answers, ways to communicate civilly about them, and how to evaluate their efficacy.

In other words, we need to be more flexible, open minded, and analytical.

Danger Six: Kids Aren't Learning Meaningful Skills and Concepts

The architects of the Common Core State Standards (as well as the proponents of spreading them all over the country) have a very effective, yet completely false mantra: The standards will end the "mile wide and inch deep" problem we have with many other standards and will get kids to think "fewer, clearer, higher." I really wish this were the case—I really do—but it's simply not.

The worst part is that almost every education leader or expert keeps repeating the same line to our teachers: "Common Core is here, whether you like it or not." Then, they tell teachers pleasant little tidbits of advice, like this: don't worry about covering *all* of the standards. You won't have time and it will keep your kids from learning higher and deeper. Here's the problem with that. The standardized tests that are aligned to Common Core subjects *do* cover all of those standards. So do the interim tests and benchmark tests, and reading comprehension tests and writing literacy tests and end-of-grade tests and the field tests.

As mentioned before, value-added measures are increasingly being added to teacher evaluations in most states. If a teacher doesn't "cover" every standard in the list, the test scores will drop. What happens to that teacher?

But even more important (and devastating), what happens to the kids? Challenge yourself to visit a typical classroom that is working under the iron fist of the Common Core standards in English/language arts or mathematics, because it's always best to see the evidence for yourself. You will see a teacher working hard to make learning happen, but with the threat of evaluative test scores hovering like a cirrus cloud. (Cirrus clouds, for those who lost their middle school Earth science vocabulary, signal incoming stormy weather.) This teacher may truly lead her students to all types of success, now and in the future, but the only thing that matters to our government—the culminating event and the intrusive must-have in a classroom—is the preparation for the constant stream of high-stakes testing.

Even when our children are exposed to the amazing lessons that talented teachers bring to their classrooms, the test becomes the be-all-to-end-all. That's how the Common Core Network is set up. That's just how it is. As Lisa Michelle Nielsen (no relation to yours truly) says, "our politicians are forcing outdated drill, kill, [and] bubble-fill tests upon our children and if the teachers don't support this we lose hundreds of millions of dollars." We also risk losing our kids.

Even the safe haven we all know as Kindergarten (and pretty soon, pre-K), where children go to learn social skills through play, interaction with other students, being read to, exploration of the environment, and other basic human skills has been turned upside-down as a result of the Common Core Network. The training for standardized testing starts early, and it's compounded by the unrealistic goals set by the architects of the CCSS. As one article suggests, blocks, playtime, music, sharing, puzzles, and coloring have been replaced with paragraph structure, tally charts, math diagrams, algebraic thinking, and expository writing.

Teachers have reported extreme anxiety, acting out, crying, fighting, and depression in their students. Many states have policies that not only label schools themselves with letter grades, but also are starting to label 4- and 5- year-olds as "novice," "emergent," "practitioner," and "expert." Most Kindergartners don't have any idea what those words mean; yet they are wearing those badges, which determine how good they are in school.

In mid-January of 2013, Dartmouth University chose to discontinue its offerings of course credit to AP students in high school, due to the fact that their course offerings are more rigorous than the supposed AP class equivalents.[6] This is an important move for higher education—and an important message for K-12 education. What Dartmouth has told the governing bodies of public schools, as well as the very high-grossing College Board, is that when you force your students to

105

"drill, kill, and bubble-fill" for a whole semester, they are most certainly *not* "college-ready." I fully expect other higher education institutions to follow suit. Will we finally find that the Common Core Network has duped us after it's too late?

Danger Seven: Computer adaptive tests are invalid

I was troubled last year to find out that my students were going to be taking an Accuplacer exam in middle school to determine which students were ready for Algebra I classes. The Accuplacer is what is known as a computer adaptive test (CAT). Now, the end-of-year summative tests being aligned with the Common Core State Standards by two consortia of assessment companies (SBAC and PARCC) are touting their tests as breakthroughs in education. Why? Because those tests, too, are CATs. What does this mean?

A computer adaptive test is designed to follow the ability level of a student as he takes the test. Every time the student answers an item correctly, the test automatically gives him a new, more challenging item to answer. On the other hand, if the student answers incorrectly, the test gives him an easier item. These are often used as placement exams for colleges and universities (like the Accuplacer), but can they be used to determine proficiency for grades 3 through 8 reading and math?

Assessment expert, Jem Muldoon, explains that these assessments are not appropriate for this purpose.[7] As students begin to get answers wrong, they will soon notice the items getting easier and easier. This becomes what is known as the "man vs. test" phenomenon, where the test taker becomes defeated by the test design itself, rather than the lack of knowledge of the content. This psychological challenge adds another variable to the test, which further invalidates it.

Also, these tests do not allow students to review their answers before finishing the tests, which is unique among high-stakes summative tests. Since the tests are progressive and adaptive, they do not allow for a student to flag responses and review them as needed. These problems lead to a cascade effect, where a student may become anxious or assumed to have failed before the test is complete. To summarize, CATs are simply unfair and highly unscientific.

Danger Eight: Kids Are Suffering Mental and Physical Distress

When standardized testing becomes the focus of classroom instruction, two groups of kids are especially badly affected: students for whom English is a second language and students who have special instructional needs. The Common Core State Standards don't take any of those needs into account and the testing policies force everyone to assess the same skills. While testing modifications do attempt to make the actual test-taking effort more accommodating for those with special needs, it still misses the point. Using common assessments for all students doesn't work, and that's been shown many times for many years.

After I told a story about an honors-level high school sophomore who was relieved to leave her test-obsessed high school and begin homeschooling, I received a message from a reader:

Dear Kris, I was very much like [this student] in school. Worked myself to death to do well. I did not miss school for fear of getting way behind — for that I was lucky. I think you are missing the bigger problem. [That student] needs help and balance in her life. She is headed for a downhill spiral — if not in high school, then college. I know. Life cannot be all about grades and school although you would have never convinced me of that.

This message reminded me that the higher-performing students are suffering, too. Honors classes used to be more open and allowed students to spread their intellectual wings. Now, they just get more homework, more vocabulary practice, and more tests.

Students are reporting mental distress, physical illness, and exhaustion due to the tests and their preparation. Again, this is not academic rigor; this is busywork at its worst. Homework is an issue outside of the scope of this book, but it is a common complaint among students who know they are being given too much of it. At a time when music, arts, PE, drama, and other exploratory activities are being cut, now students are forced to cut their own personal time in order to maintain their homework schedules. In other words, kids—who should have more free time to play and socialize and move and exercise and discover— now have no lives outside of their school duties. All in the name of raising test scores.

Some would say that this type of education is what the Common Core Network was designed for—to get our kids used to the idea of working long hours doing menial work, since that's what the wealthy elite wants from our public training programs. I don't know if I agree or disagree with that suggestion, but I do know that our current schooling leads to troubling things to come.

Kids who can't handle the stress and the pace end up being labeled ADD, ADHD, or "exceptional." In the decade since NCLB was enacted, clinical cases of ADD and ADHD have skyrocketed, and while the studies are not necessarily a confirmation of causal evidence, there is a very strong correlation between increasing incidence of testing (and the culture of test prep) and the number of cases of these conditions. Kids who don't score high enough are labeled as "not proficient" or "approaching proficiency" or "emerging." Regardless of the label, the kids are smart enough to figure out that they aren't cutting it. Then, the self-fulfilling prophecy kicks in and it's all downhill from there: "The tests say I'm a failure, so I guess that's what I am."

When kids feel hopeless, they check out. When they check out for long enough, they eventually leave. Our government's only responses to high dropout rates are punitive: laws that raise mandatory schooling age, truancy charges against parents, and enrollment into alternative schools (some of which work very well; some of which don't).

The Common Core Network guarantees more frustration, stress, burnout, illness, and dropout students. In fact, according to research from several experts, standards of any kind, which prescribe certain benchmarks by grade, age, or class, stifle learning. It's not only documented, but also common sense that kids develop in different ways, at different times, and can then do different things in different ways. Remember, the Common Core State Standards come from two lawyers and a consortium of leaders representing Corporate America. The network is designed to stifle, much like the training structures in the middle-class workforce. So, if training workers is what we're going for, then you're probably buying into the Common Core Network as "the silver bullet." (It's going to make your investor friends some cash too!)

Our kids are being treated as data points in a large-scale statistics experiment, and their lives are being recorded and filed with testing companies, the government, and others, without parent or student permission or knowledge of that data's use. Most parents don't know that. This is one the worst parts of the whole Common Core Network scheme, in my opinion: my child's personal and educational data is being collected, archived, shared, sold, and traded by the likes of the Gates Foundation—

without my permission.[8] And at the expense of their learning, motivation, and engagement. What do the students have to say about that?

5

The Real Education Crisis[1]

"Education is what remains when one has forgotten what one has learned in school."

- Albert Einstein

As was mentioned in the first chapter, one of the most important types of qualitative input that we habitually ignore is the student voice, a phenomenon that Nikhil Goyal calls the adult table vs. kid table of the education conversation.[2] When a late elementary student says, "I don't like school," we believe that the proper adult response is, "Well, I'm sorry. We all have to do things we don't like." Think about that answer for a minute. Think about what was just said to a child. We're telling our young people—who are born and are hardwired to be curious, natural learners—that they are expected to push and suffer through a system that takes their natural dispositions and reverses them through a systematic process that will leave them with little curiosity or motivation; a process we call school. And they have to do it, whether they like it or not. Many of those students already live in situations that limit their wills, their spirits, and their abilities to "be a kid."

Middle school has been implied as "the great killer of creativity" by many of my colleagues and students. I disagree, after having observed several elementary school classrooms recently. The Common Core State Standards have been forced onto grades Kindergarten through 12, and all of those grades now have standardized testing requirements. Those states that have applied for Race to the Top grants and have adopted the Common Core State Standards are seeing early elementary students testing at least 3 times a year, not including field and benchmark tests.

The Common Core Network has created the presets for dropout kids earlier than ever. Middle school's stigma has been shifted back a few years, as elementary kids now come home exhausted, demoralized, and loaded down with homework. First graders are coming home in tears because they don't want to take that big test everyone keeps pressuring them about. They are tired of doing worksheet after worksheet, as their schools attempt to get them ready to test on skills they aren't developmentally ready for. (Check the copyright notice on the worksheets your kid brings home. There are pretty good odds it came from a Pearson test preparation product that was sold to the school district.)

School has become a dead zone for kids (which makes it easy to see why they love video games and social networking so much). Children have tons of disposable energy and a real enthusiasm for the things around them. As adults, we've grown out of (or have been trained out of) that natural tendency to notice everything around us and ask questions about those things. Toddlers ask why constantly. Young children ask how. Older children ask what if. They want to be stimulated and they deserve to be. School should be a place where our kids are happy to be and happy to learn. It should be our jobs as parents and teachers to allow our children to explore their paths of discovery, rather than cowing to a rigid system and forcing them to stay on the narrow, straight line that we call the Common Core State Standards.

The Common Core Network is especially troubling for students who have learning disabilities, are English language learners, or who live in abject poverty. Sonja, a first-generation American in 8th grade, told me often that she was scared that her family might have to go back to Mexico if their visas couldn't be renewed. What worried her even more was what her teachers kept telling her about her reading scores. According to the Common Core, Sonja had to show proficiency in standards that forced her to read material that was unfamiliar to her in her second language and her second culture.

Sonja showed incredible progress through her middle school career, according to her teachers: her fluency improved, her comprehension was fantastic, and her ability to use several different texts to draw conclusions and compare and contrast were up to par with her classmates. When she took the 8th grade end-of-the-year state assessment, she started feeling sick to her stomach and had to be excused several times. She told her teachers afterwards that she became very nervous because the test's reading passages and multiple-choice responses were not like the types of skills she had mastered. The tests, she said, had passages that she couldn't understand, since there was no context, yet she was expected to be able to read, analyze, and infer based on those pieces of text in order to show that she was proficient. She had become very good at using many different texts to come to conclusions, yet the tests of the Common Core Network don't assess for this important skill.

Researchers have criticized the tendency of the Common Core to keep students "in the text," meaning they should not be expected to use their prior knowledge or any other text to supplement the learning. This is a very dangerous idea, since it teaches our kids to stick to one text and derive all opinions and ideas from it. Most teachers I've talked to refuse to teach this way, and instead practice "triangulation," where students find at least three different texts on the same topic to seek bias, infer author meaning, and compare ideas. Strangely, the Standards themselves ask for this, but the teaching materials and standardized tests do not emphasize divergent thinking, and instead give students one right answer to choose, where several opinions may be seen. As language acquisition specialist, Stephen Krashen, repeatedly suggests, we need to let these kids read. Not the stuff that the Common Core system prescribes, but whatever they want. You want kids to learn how to read, write, think, and analyze? Get out of the way for a little while and just let them read.[3]

Here are few more cases of kids who just want to learn, without the pressure to perform on meaningless and harmful tests.

Joe

Kids with learning disabilities are treated even more unfairly. Two of my students in the past three years have had dyslexia, on top of other deficiencies that made learning new material challenging for them. One of them, Joe, had the type of imagination that both Hollywood and MIT would fight over. Joe was full of *what ifs*, especially after learning something especially interesting in science or history class. Joe spent several hours per week in the library researching and reading, trying to build up the necessary background knowledge to see if his amazing ideas were realistic or could be attempted.

Unfortunately, Joe also had some difficulties with his reading fluency. His speech and vision disorders played a part in this, and he tried very hard to work past those challenges. After taking his 7th grade end-of-year reading test, he was told that he would need to attend tutoring from his English/language arts teacher three days a week in order to improve his test scores. Joe could no longer spend those hours pursuing his own curiosities and innovations. Joe was now forced to prepare to try to raise his score on a test that doesn't measure his intelligence or his aptitude or his creativity or his drive. Joe got quieter during his 8th grade year. He didn't ask as many questions. And he started missing more school.

Kayla

High schools that have fully implemented the Common Core Network are probably the worst possible institutions for adolescent minds in this era (assuming those kids managed to hold on to their motivation and inspiration all the way to this point). The speed of technology, and the resulting ready access to information makes just about every day of a standardized curriculum completely obsolete in American high schools.

Kayla is a 10th grader at a middle-of-the-road high school in a suburban area. She considers herself a high-performing student who always gets good grades and high scores. She plans to get a terminal degree in neuroscience and run for Congress.

118

She overcame reading difficulties in elementary school to grow into a top student who loves to read about anything that catches her interest. Her high school adopted the Common Core State Standards and high-stakes benchmark assessments less than two years ago. According to Kayla:

> *From my experience, a normal school day consists of the following: copying notes, listening to lectures, filling out worksheets, reviewing for tests, taking tests, and receiving an overload of homework. Then we do it again the next day, and the next, and the next...*

This echoes Line Dalile's assessment of high school, and you can see that we are killing not only their curiosity, but also their reasons to be in school at all. Kids know when they aren't learning, and this isn't just about school being fun (although I think that it should be—when kids enjoy what they're doing, they'll learn). These kids are smart enough to know they are being strung along in order to make someone's numbers look good.

Kayla continued, to make the point that she knows she being cheated out of an education:

> *We are spoonfed unit after unit of information, but we are not taught how to process or use it. Most of it is forgotten. And the students know this, they ask things like, "when in my life am I going to use the equation of a hyperbola?" The most honest answer I've heard from a teacher is that you're not. You do math to learn how to*

memorize and work things out. So why not just teach us how to memorize and work things out? There's no need for useless formulas and equations were going to forget after we pass the tests. Better yet, why not teach us something useful? Perhaps instead of having us memorize an equation, we are taught why the equation works; if we are taught why, not only math but in any subject, we can then begin to understand things more clearly and apply the things we've learned. I don't just want to learn facts; I want to learn useful life skills.

As a former math teacher, I can tell you that doing math to learn how to memorize is about as counterproductive as you can get. However, that's about as far as this curriculum goes. Interestingly, the Common Core State Standards have the right idea here: students should be able to build equations and understand the information within. However, looking at the list of standards that must be taught and mastered by the time the standardized tests roll around, you can see how a teacher feels the pressure to front-load equations, make his students memorize them, and know in what situations to use them. This is the type of practice that leads students to memorize things until the test has passed, after which they dump all of that clutter to make room for new facts and formulas.

Memorizing equations, formulas, and facts in this technological era makes no sense. Almost every student in a school building has this information within arms reach at all times. Critics will say, "I had to memorize this stuff, so today's kids should too." Just because we had to suffer, they should too? Why would we purposely stifle our kids' potential by making them memorize and then forget these tools, when a high school student can easily find them within seconds using technology? And why do we not allow our teachers to teach the process, the applications, and the synthesis of important ideas, rather than pressuring them with arbitrary, all-or-nothing timelines? These are questions we need to think about more carefully.

Kayla has more questions, which are important:

> *Can you imagine a scenario where it doesn't have to be a legal requirement to go to school; where kids are willing to go because they want to? Many kids enjoy the social aspect of school, but dislike the "learning" part: the grades, the testing, and the lectures. Why is this? Is it by nature that kids just don't want to learn? Are we born willing to be ignorant? If this were true, there wouldn't be as many frustrated parents, tired from answering all of their toddlers' questions. Children always want to know more. We are born with an eagerness to learn and to understand the world around us; so why is there generally an opposing attitude associated with school, a place of learning? There are many reasons for this, and maybe it's not the kids fault they don't enjoy going to school.*

It's not their fault. Kids love going to school, if school has something to offer. A famous line from Zack Morris, the lead character in the 80s teen show, *Saved by the Bell*, tells us that kids "love school; it's too bad classes get in the way." This was said on TV to get a laugh, but it's not funny anymore. It's so common that it's problematic for all of our kids, including the kids who were always seen as gifted or highly performing.

Finally, Kayla offered some thoughts that are reminiscent of what constructivists have been saying for decades:

Another problem with school is that it is not at all personalized. Even though it's known that people learn at different rates, we are all still put in a grade classified by our age and expected to follow along at the same pace as the teaching. The pacing of schooling is often too fast or too slow for the majority of the students; very rarely is it just right.

Not only do we learn at different rates, we also learn in different ways. An assignment that requires a student to draw a picture for every vocabulary word might not work for someone who learns by reading. In the same way, an assignment where a student is required to write a definition for every vocabulary word would be a waste of time for someone who learns best visually. Students should have more freedom in the way they learn. Forcing work that doesn't help a student only wastes their time and causes even more of a disinterest in the class. However, with the current school system, giving more freedom wouldn't fully fix the problem. Students would find a way to get away with doing as little as possible if they designed their own work, and teachers don't have the time to personally help each student to prevent this.

The Common Core Network has made students' learning difficult by standardizing it. As Kayla said, everyone learns differently and different interests spark different students. Secretary Arne Duncan gave great lip service to the ideas of differentiation and personalized learning, but since he's not a teacher, he had no idea what those terms meant. Personalized learning, for him and his friends, means tracking individual student test data, planning interventions accordingly, and then tracking the results. This is not personalized learning, this is norm-referenced data compilation and ranking.

Personalized learning means that students' abilities, interests, and ideas lead them and the curricula to goals that have been set by students, teachers, and parents. The alternative, which is what Secretary Duncan talks about, is a database of test scores that advises which students are ahead of the curve and which students need interventions to catch up—all while being taught and tested out of the same material, using identical methods.

So, why aren't we using more personalized learning techniques? As Kayla pointed out, there simply is no time. I remember a time when the movement to allow students to set the pace for their learning was growing, and teachers and students saw massive improvements in engagement, motivation, knowledge acquisitions, vocabulary building, reading skills, and critical thinking. Even teachers who weren't comfortable at first saw the successes and wanted to learn how to be part of it. Now that standardized testing against a common set of flawed standards has taken over, test preparation and the tests themselves have cut deeply into real learning time. What is the fix (according to the Common Core Network)? Longer school days and years and, oddly, larger class sizes.

Kayla is bored and frustrated. So are her peers. Our advice to Kayla so far is, "Just deal with it. It will be over in a few years." From toddler to teenager, do we ever feel like we should stop placating our kids and actually do something to help them grow?

Michael

Michael is a very socially aware high school student who wants to change the world. He is fiercely independent and wants to be a philanthropist, as well as someone who can advise public policy, someday. His frustration with school comes from his teachers' inability to truly teach their students:

Students ask teachers how to apply their knowledge. But, [the students] are ignored. For them, it isn't about practical application; it is about a test score. Though that may not be entirely their fault, some accept it and, as a result, fail as a teacher.

It sounds harsh, but this does portray a student's frustration. Students have been pushed aside as the Common Core Network requires less interaction and more data, and they don't know whom to blame. When the entire school day is spent with their teachers, that's where students project their frustrations and may call them boring, incompetent, or careless.

Michael does this as he reflects on his interactions with the adults he trusts to guide him in his pursuit of deeper meaning and knowledge. He's obviously disappointed, as seen here:

I actually get sad upon interacting with teachers. They generally believe they are the best at what they do and they are unable to see things in different perspectives. On top of that, thanks to the society they've grown in, they are always right: "Are you a teacher? Did you go to college to learn how to teach? You don't know what you're talking about." Even if they care, they fail to understand the fact that they too are students. The tendency to disregard this is what causes their failings as a teacher. Instead of listening, then adjusting, they teach in their same ways.

I will back this statement up with my own observations of *some* teachers, but by no means many. The saddest part of this is that students and teachers have become distrustful of each other in this new environment. When the results of standardized tests advise all decisions, it turns out to be a wicked game of student vs. teacher, teacher vs. administrator, and administrator vs. the state. Branching from that comes parent vs. teacher and parent vs. student. It's a caustic pool of competition and animosity that now fills the hallways of our schools, and it's becoming more and more palpable.

With a few, important exceptions, many students have reported to me that they don't trust their teachers as people who can help them with problems; students don't feel respected, they get yelled at too much, and they don't feel challenged to use their own minds at school. Again, this isn't the teachers', students' or parents' fault. This is the environment that education reform has created under the Common Core Network.

In Chapter One, I described what kids need from us, the adults in their lives. It's obvious that the environments we have in place are not working. The Common Core Network (and its predecessors) has created a toxic blend of national standards, low funding, overtesting, and a teacher corps of temporary workers. It especially affects the kids who live in poor, urban and rural communities. Members of the Common Core Network will tell us that poor, minority kids and their families will thank us for this formula. Let's talk about that.

6

A Cure for Poverty?

"Far less wealthy industrialized countries have committed to end child poverty, while the United States is sliding backwards. We can do better. We must demand that our leaders do better."

- Marian Wright Edelman

The Common Core Network had a specific target in mind even before all the pieces started coming together. The standards were written, the testing structure was designed, and the investors were wringing their hands. This is the perfect crime, because it's easy to create a shining image of sainthood for the perpetrators, and it turned out to be easy to trick people into voting for legislation that gives the Network all the power and money they want. The target? Low-income, urban schools with minority populations, high dropout rates, and low test scores. Money from low-income schools and poor people, you ask? Really?

Absolutely. The Federal government spends a lot of money on low-income schools. Investors want that money, which means they need a system to get it (vouchers and private charter schools).[1] Investors want the best return on the lowest initial investment (inexpensive school curricula and cheap labor, such as Teach for America teachers). There are two logical (yet fundamentally different) ways to approach the income-based achievement gap: (1) raise the test scores of poor students or (2) fix the poverty itself. Which do you think has the best return-on-investment, especially in the short term? Consider the following.

As I mentioned earlier, education reformers have designed a system that ensures failure, as measured by standardized testing, for low-income schools and districts. The movement has had the ultimate goal of privatizing and commodifying K-12 schools for quite awhile—at least a few decades. They keep running into the same roadblock, however, which has thwarted their efforts: most American parents don't want their kids' schools run by corporations. Most parents have the foresight to realize that when business interests control their children's learning, those interests are only geared for what's good for business, not what's good for kids.

So, the privatization movement had to find a better way. It's actually pretty brilliant, even in its selfishness and harmful means. The new game plan? Create an environment where parents ultimately lose faith and confidence in the public schools so that they will demand other choices. When parents demand things (and when propagandists amplify those demands), those in charge of the system tend to listen. And that's not a bad thing; parents should be the voice that creates change and progress. These are our kids. We fight for them every day. But, now, we're being played and our kids and we are pawns in a game of divide and conquer.

We have been consistently reminded in the media that our kids are the lowest performing in the world when it comes to reading, math, and science. StudentsFirst, Michelle Rhee's organization, reminds us that students deserve better, and if the schools won't provide better, we must fire them. All of this hype is based on the NAEP performance of American 8th grade students as compared to their counterparts. This data, at a glance, does show cause for concerns a call for action. However, it also calls for an opportunity to ask a lot of questions (we seemed to have skipped that part, as we tend to do). One such question should be, and has been, "*Who* is not performing, and why?" We've answered that question by state and by region, using results from the NAEP test, which is randomly administered to 4th, 8th, and 12th graders. It has to go deeper than that.

Here's where it starts to get more interesting. If the data from NAEP is broken down by Title I participation, it becomes clear quickly that our students who live in relative affluence are outperforming their peers in other countries, hands down. Our students who are participating in Title I, especially minority students, lag far behind, hence the oft-cited "achievement gap." Indeed, this problem was obvious back in the 1960s, when the Elementary and Secondary Education Act (ESEA) was passed in order to try to equalize the educational playing field and protect poor and minority students. The first section, Title I, called for increased resources for those schools serving low-income populations in order to close the that achievement gap. If you average the scale scores of all students in the U.S.—poor, middle class, and wealthy—you see our alarming current place in the world, the way that the media reports it. This sort of shows how statistics can be used to bend the truth, if you really want them to.

Proponents of the Common Core Network have repeatedly offered the following talking points: "Education is the road out of poverty," and "Poverty does not equal destiny."[2] These are wildly popular and feel-good rally cries, but they have no backing in reality. Sure, there are success stories of kids who have somehow found the will or the help of a mentor to pull themselves from the crushing world of poverty, pushed themselves to the limit, and then rose above expectations to reach their goals. But, these are anecdotes. The majority of students who live in poverty cannot escape those circumstances, and that's mostly because they find themselves severely limited by those circumstances.

Many students who qualify for Title I services also qualify for free or reduced lunches, free after school care (where available), Medicaid, and food stamps. In other words, these kids are poor, often hungry, and cannot afford health care. In fact, over 20% of American children live in poverty and almost half of all children live in low-income families.[3] That is the highest those percentages have been since the 1950s; and are the highest percentages of any modern, industrial nation. Fully half of kids who spend their childhoods in poverty will remain in poverty at age 35, due to less access to higher education, and higher incidence of incarceration, drug and alcohol addiction, and other poverty-related factors.

It's popularly known that high-stakes testing is more of a measure of affluence and demographics than of educational achievement.[4] The Common Core State Standards are designed to be measured using norm-referenced tests, where students are ranked among each other and against global counterparts. This would work just fine, if every student learned the same way, the same material, at the same time, and lived in similar circumstances. The Common Core Network assumes all four, but only attempts to create an environment for identical materials and timing. Even then, it attempts to rank students on how well they take in prescribed knowledge in preparation for future careers.

When a student who lives in poverty is distracted by the social and economic distractions inherent, she falls victim to a set of potential outcomes that wealthier students do not. Access to outside resources (Internet, books, tutoring, etc.) is extremely limited, as is access to adults with higher education. Wealthier students are afforded more time outside the home to experience enriching activities. Wealthier students generally have better access to healthcare, nutrition, and mental health providers. Finally, wealthier students do not generally have the same life stressors that low-income students have.

I've seen the difference, as has any other teacher. Our poorer kids worry about things that more affluent kids don't think twice about. I've had students come to me, crying, because they weren't sure they would be living in their home a week from then. Some have told me they were so tired because their parents were up late fighting about the bills or jobs or childcare. Several students have one or both parents in jail for crimes related to poverty. My wealthier students smile more than their poorer counterparts, and they get in less trouble for behavior problems stemming from situations that young people don't know how to deal with.

Then, after struggling with all of that, test time comes. The school does its best to feed everyone and prepare them for the grueling schedule. We encourage our students to get a good night's sleep, do something relaxing in the morning, eat a good breakfast, and show up to school early. Our encouragement and ideas only go so far. We have no control past that.

One of my 8th grade girls told me on the day of a state test that she had been up until 3 a.m. trying to comfort her sick younger brother, because mom had to work the graveyard shift. It's the only job her mom could find and the only thing that keeps them living in their one-bedroom apartment and not in their small car. She was exhausted, but hopeful. She was one of my most committed and curious students. She tried hard every day to show me, and herself, that she was smart enough to understand math.

She didn't "pass" the test. She ended up with a "nearing proficiency" rank and fell into the 35th percentile. Even with the encouragement she felt in class and the progress she was making in math reasoning, she simply could not focus on that three-hour snapshot test of what she was supposed to be able to memorize.

Many school districts, including mine at the time, prescribe teacher tutoring as a tool to help students like this girl. What they're really asking is to make sure the kids who didn't pass the benchmarks tests are spending more time in classroom seats, memorizing the things they couldn't before. Most of my time as a tutor was spent on making sure my students spent enough time on formula procedure so that it became second nature for a while—just long enough to pass the test. After the pressure of the test was over, I would gamble that not even half of my students could regurgitate the formulas and procedures I had asked them to memorize, and I can't think of any reason they should have to.

The Common Core State Standards are strongly pushed to be adopted by states in which there is a large population living in poverty because there is no other feasible way to receive desperately needed Race to the Top money. Unfortunately, no matter how many "innovations" a district or state comes up with, none but a few of them will meet the expectations that come with the grant money. Race to the Top has two confounding rules that are working fiercely against the narrowing of the achievement gap: adoption of the Common Core State Standards and regular standardized testing. Together, these make school very difficult for teachers to teach, frustrating for students to learn, and pointless for students who have little hope or reason to be there in the first place.

I posted on my blog the following as a tongue-in-cheek look at the real innovations that school systems should adopt if they want to see their Title I funds for their low-income schools:

> *The only Common Core resources you need to meet the demands of Race to the Top are:*
>
> > *1. Military-style discipline and classroom structure (talking and playing are time-wasters)*
> > *2. Practice worksheets and workbooks to fill the endless hours of drill-and-kill busy work (provided by your friendly Pearson distributor)*

3. More time in classrooms practicing low-level skills in preparation for the monthly tests (at the expense of arts, music, recess, and even lunch breaks)

4. An evaluation process that keeps teachers in line (there is no time to develop our kids as human beings when we have so little time to train them as workers)

5. New technology that supports the perpetual test practice, as well as the tests themselves, that will soon be required (oh, and the districts need to pay for those)

You want your RttT grant money? You better get busy. Sure, in the end, you'll have spent way more than the Federal government will give you, but that's why you were supposed to come up innovative ideas on how to get all of your kids to "high-growth."

Satire is fun, as long it's not uncomfortably close to the truth. Unfortunately, this is way too close. Walk through the halls of any school run by the Common Core Network and you'll find the evidence. Walk through any Title I funded school, and that evidence becomes glaring and haunting.

The Common Core Network has an assumption about low-income students that is both unrealistic and insulting: you can get these kids to achieve higher if you keep setting the bar higher, testing them constantly to make sure they're getting there, and then punishing their teachers and schools when things don't move fast enough. The Common Core Network doesn't advocate for better resources, better teacher evaluation systems, more money for nutrition and healthcare, more learning activities, or a more well-rounded education. The Common Core Network advocates for one thing and one thing only: getting kids "college and career ready," as evidenced only by their performance on high-stakes tests. "College and career ready" is happy talk for ranking and filing our next generation of high school graduates.

The truth is, we've handed our poor kids' futures to privatizers because fixing the real problem is apparently too hard and goes against the interests of the wealthy (we've already almost privatized food stamps and temporary assistance for needy families, as private banks now administer and track those funds). It's disturbing to hear this, since it's obvious that in order to truly close the achievement gap, *we need to get rid of poverty first*, not the other way around. It's much more likely that lifting kids out of poverty first will lead to a narrowed achievement gap. I don't recall where I heard the wisdom that the best education reform legislation in the last 50 years is the Affordable Care Act (i.e. Obamacare), because it suggests the expansion of Medicaid to all families living under the poverty level. Healthy kids are generally more highly engaged and happy, and therefore more prepared to learn in school. It's not the end of child health problems, by any stretch of the imagination, but it's certainly a start to fixing them.

Instead, again, corporate education reform not only dismisses poverty as a cause for learning gaps, but blatantly denies it. Instead, we close schools that can't meet arbitrary goals, fire their staffs, and shuffle the students elsewhere. Charter school operators step in here, and offer a silver bullet: a structured, "no excuses," and highly disciplined system where the promise of high standardized test achievement is gospel.

Public schools are being admonished for not being able to close the standardized-test achievement gap. There is a growing movement by charter school operators and "reformers" to allow privately run, public-funded charter schools to take over this problem and fix it with "revolutionary" methods. Unfortunately, many of these schools have done little more than select students with potential, militarize and standardize the classroom experience, and punish students who make excuses or do not perform. When a student does not adapt well to the strict control of the charter school, he is removed from that system and returned to the public school system. While this may sound reasonable, it is a cycle that has spun out of control to the benefit of charters and the chagrin of traditional schools. It seems that the most aggressive solutions are coming from the non-educators—the people who have a pretty good sense on how to make some quick money, but little to no idea how to educate and prepare kids.

The Bill Gates Solution

I remember a time when Bill Gates, the founder of the Microsoft Corporation, was considered the smartest man in the world. I always wondered what exactly earned him that kind of respect. I know that he revolutionized the computing world, as we knew it (of course, he just happened to be lucky, I think; many others were doing comparable things in his day). I think most people put him on such a pedestal because he became an ultra-billionaire doing it. Money is power and can buy a lot of respect in America.

It turns out that Bill Gates isn't all that smart, and he has no educational training whatsoever. He has traveled the world, observing poverty, hunger, and other human maladies, and the best he has been able to come up with is "measurement." Now, don't get me wrong, I believe that data is extremely important when trying to get to the bottom of things and trying to find ways to fix complex and stubborn problems. But, I don't believe that objective measurement is the solution to everything, especially problems that are made up.

Mr. Gates has decided that computerized measurement of children's learning is the best route to take to make poor and minority students in America more globally competitive. He has consistently called for larger class sizes (in a time when our classrooms are already overflowing) and computer-based learning. The latter can hardly be a surprise, since his corporation stands in a position to be a major player in it. And larger class sizes can only be explained by his desire to see flesh-and-blood teachers replaced by those computers.[5]

Bill Gates misses the point of education. (Maybe he doesn't; his own kids are part of a learning community that will *never* be run the way he wants to see low-income public schools run.) His prescriptions for computer-based education take out variables that are demonstrably important to kids, namely relationships with teachers and other adults at school, as well as meaningful interactions with peers. I have seen the computer-based model during test preparation in public schools and it is truly depressing. It's quiet, impersonal, and long. Kids are exhausted at the end of the day, and they remember very little.

The debate I've been watching and participating in for some time, with other professionals, seems to always come back to the idea that our kids need a balance. Technology is one of the most important assets in our schools when it's used as a tool of learning. It can also be considered one of the most damaging factors when it becomes the only tool. One-to-one laptop initiatives are an exciting idea, knowing that every student has the power at their fingertips to quickly research, collaborate, and become a global citizen. They are also scary idea when we consider how quickly they can be misused to isolate students behind a screen, as they move through modules of pre-recorded, on-screen instruction and take quizzes in preparation for standardized tests.

Bill Gates has attempted to validate his findings and beliefs by suggesting that standardized tests are only one of a few different methods of evaluation (students surveys and observations are also discussed), but all results are only validated in Gates' study by how closely they align to test scores. This line of reasoning is almost identical to that of Michelle Rhee, who is more than happy to have Bill Gates in her wealthy "philanthropist" collection. You know, the people who are so much smarter than poor people and therefore know what's best for them.

Measurement should happen, by all means. The problem with the Gates idea is that he believes everything should be measured objectively, namely teacher effectiveness. Many important things in a school building can't be evaluated on simple, objective metrics, no matter how badly Mr. Gates wants them to be.

Knowledge is Power

According to the Knowledge is Power Program, now known as KIPP schools, it takes "a balanced approach to education: hard work and a strong academic curriculum balanced with the development of the character strengths needed to succeed in college and in life." Anyone will agree that it sounds great, and most charter schools have similar beliefs. What warrants our critical thinking and pause are the promises of achievement for low-income students and the ongoing war cry that "education is the path out of poverty."

Many charter schools boast high achievement rates (although this has been contested repeatedly) and graduation rates from large charters have been impressive. On the down side, attrition rates are high (up to 40% for KIPP) and college success rates are much lower than even charters would like to see (33% of KIPP alumni graduate from college). Add to that the teacher attrition rate, where about half of KIPP's teachers leave every year, either to pursue other professions or due to job dissatisfaction. About half of KIPP's teachers are Teach for America alumni, which means that teaching is a temporary job for them anyway.[6]

Standardized test scores are *the* measure of achievement when comparing charters to conventional schools, and there is no statistically significant difference here. Charter schools that are set up in urban, low-income, and minority neighborhoods have placed themselves in the position of providing hope of success, where before there was none. The numbers simply don't support that this goal has been met. But it's even worse than that.[7]

KIPP's motto is "Work hard. Be nice." This is a great marketing slogan. However, this isn't going to ensure success for kids who really want to go college. The statistics for KIPP mirror (and exaggerate, in some cases) the same problems that the leaders of the Common Core Network complain so loudly about conventional public schools. The model may be different; the results really aren't. Granted, KIPP does allow time for music, art, and other electives, since students are at school for an average of 9.5 hours a day. Other than that, now that conventional schools have adopted the Common Core State Standards and the multitude of tests to accompany them, the two types of schools will soon be indistinguishable: strict, quiet, competitive, punitive, and measured by tests.

To summarize the KIPP ideal: higher test scores equal college success and an escape from poverty. It simply doesn't make logical sense to begin with, and the data certainly doesn't support it. And, just like their conventional counterparts, KIPP and other charter school students are being robbed of a motivating, engaging, exploratory, and enriching education.

It's difficult to find official survey data from KIPP schools, since they are very protective and defensive about their data, so here are a few student tweets from a recently trending conversation from the hashtag #onlykippkids:

> "[They] have the school buildings made of aluminum & shaped windows with gates looking like a prison."
>
> "feel like our schools a prison lol...it really is."
>
> "Never seen whitepeople at our school..."
>
> "have no kind of FREEDOM."

Another KIPP student tweets a photo of an article that suggests that teens need time to relax and get plenty of sleep. She captioned it: "#KIPP needs to realize this."

Unfortunately, the hashtag no longer brings up any conversations. It is very difficult to get student reviews of experiences at KIPP schools. I wish that weren't the case. Students should be encouraged to speak more about their school experiences—what they like, what they want to change. Honest, open opinions (after all, if KIPP is doing such great things, why do we only hear from a few, select, super-successful students?). The two students I spoke to personally made me realize that the "Be Nice" half of the motto was in reference to their discipline, which is based on a system of demerits. One student told me that her teachers always spoke about rewards for positive behavior, but she never saw any of those rewards, and she was a good student.

I refuse to say that KIPP and other charter organizations like it are bad for all kids, because that would be dishonest. KIPP portrays very prominently its star students and those who have succeeded past their schooling there. I just wish KIPP would be more honest about its success rates and where it needs to improve.

What I have to say, however, is that KIPP does more harm than good. Enrollment in a charter school like KIPP is the end result of parental frustration with local public schools, and those public schools do have real problems. They are generally located in areas suffering from abject poverty, unemployment, drug trade, high crime, and an environment that does not support engagement or learning. Instead of truly trying to remedy the problems of the neighborhoods and the schools, the game plan is to punish the public schools for test results, which do not measure student achievement to begin with, and then offer families a "better alternative," for which there is no strong evidence.

What's happening now, with the Common Core and Race to the Top, is the move to turn all schools (especially inner-city schools) into KIPP-like models. The privatization movement has done a superior job convincing people that the KIPP model is the only way to get poor, minority kids into college, which means overbearing discipline, common standards, and ongoing achievement tests. This isn't learning. This isn't growing. This isn't natural. Training students to score higher on standardized tests may get them some competitive numbers and a high school diploma, but it does little to nothing to prepare them for their futures.

The corporate education reform movement comes full-circle here. This is the end game. Poor kids who drop out of high school use resources that are funded by tax dollars. The way the corporate reformers see it, if they can take in those kids and their funding, they can put them into the charter system and keep them all on a narrow path to the workforce, which leads to a spot in the labor market that Wall Street needs. Jobs are good, right?

Not if the jobs are all low-level, with no chance for growth, and students were preselected based on aptitudes that have been tracked since the 8th grade and earlier. Happiness doesn't come from data, tracking, and placements. Happiness comes from wonder, appreciation, and involvement in the community.

The manipulation of the school system to track and rank poor kids into preselected jobs is bad, since all kids should be allowed to set and work toward their own goals; that type of policy also weakens our entire nation. Recent KIPP data shows that it doesn't work anyway, with higher dropout rates than the public schools that feed those charters and low college graduation rates. But it gets worse. Much, much worse.

The School-to-Prison Pipeline[8]

My last teaching assignment was the hardest for me. The school building was half rural and half urban and almost 100% free and reduced lunch. In other words, most of these kids were living in poverty. Some of them were living in crushing poverty. Some of them had a parent in prison. Most of them had divorced parents. A few of them already had delinquency records. One or two of them had been shuffled between schools due to behaviors or other offenses.

That wasn't the hard part for me. I've taught in enough low-income schools to know that, while those types of things make teaching more challenging, they can be overcome by good teachers who respect and love them, and try to help kids get the education they deserve. What was tough for me was how they were treated. Gangs are an issue that has to be dealt with on a daily basis in many low-income areas. Many schools use uniform dress codes to address the problems of colors, symbols, and markings, which does make sense. Although I do think that there are better ways to address these issues—and that we are taking a lazy way out—this isn't my problem with the dress code.

What bugs me is that poor, urban schools are beginning to look very much like another institution, which requires strict uniformity, discipline, and following orders: prison. It sounds excessive, but it's true. Middle schools are the most depressing, as we've taken freedom away from preadolescents in the interest of "safety" and "comfort." What I really see is an attempt at staff convenience and student control. Students eat at assigned lunch tables, walk through the halls in single-file silence between classes, and are kept on a strict task schedule. During "recess," students are led single file to the field, surrounded by staff, and find their cliques. The comparison is too easy to make, and the students at KIPP can sympathize.

They're treated differently, also. Try visiting a middle school in an affluent area in any community, where there is no uniform dress code, passage between classes is free, and lunch seating is more or less open. Then, spend the next day in a middle school in a poor area and see for yourself the differences. Infractions that result in a head shake or a slap on the wrist in an affluent,

146

mostly white school are often more severely punished in poorer, mostly minority schools. A fight that results in suspension in the former can result in expulsion—even arrest—in the latter.

These are the differences between wealth and lack of wealth. These are the differences in how society views those of means and those in poverty. These are differences that lead to the conclusion that more money, more testing, and stricter discipline do not fight poverty. In fact, the more we lock down our poor schools with rules, dress codes, and a different approach to their learning, the more inevitable the fates of our kids. We have to fight poverty directly—fair wages, secure employment, health care, food, and comfortable housing for all—if we want to see these kids meet the educational expectations for which we hold them.

7

New Visions for Public Education

"The task of the educator lies in seeing that the child does not confound good with immobility and evil with activity."

- Maria Montessori

I'd like to start this chapter with a passage from my good friend, Mark Naison:

I have a very different vision of what public schools should be doing than Bill Gates, Michelle Rhee, Jeb Bush, Arne Duncan, Michael Bloomberg and the current generation of "School Reformers." My vision involves making schools centers of community revitalization where young people's curiosity and creativity is nurtured, where student differences are recognized and respected, where the physical and emotional health of children is promoted, where teachers have long careers, and where parents and community members are welcome.

I think you begin with creating a child-friendly environment. That means sharply reducing the number of tests, leaving ample room for exercise and play, giving primacy to the arts, and having instruction in subject areas, when possible, incorporating hands-on learning and project-based activity.

I would also like as many schools as possible to grow and prepare food (with indoor and outdoor farms) and link that to science instruction, have students participate in community improvement initiatives, have students use computers they can carry with them rather than forcing them to use them at desks, and become involved in mentoring younger students. As much as possible, I would like learning to be cooperative rather than competitive and extend that to the teaching staff—a process that would mean removing the threat of school closings and having evaluation done by peers using multiple measures rather than consultants deriving their data from student test scores.

I would also like to see an end to the "one path fits all" approach to secondary education and revive the vocational and technical schools (once a fixture in our educational mix) to prepare students for decent paying jobs in traditional trades, such as repair of automobiles and appliances, as well as emerging areas like solar and wind energy and environmentally friendly agriculture. Here, we can learn a great deal from how Germany and other Northern European countries do this.

Additionally, I would try to create a climate where talented people enter teaching as a lifetime career, which involves treating teachers with respect, giving them input into all decisions affecting their professional lives, including at those made at the city, state and national level, and an end to attacks on their collective bargaining rights.

And in communities which suffer the effects of poverty, I would turn schools into 24-hour community centers, which serve neighborhood residents as well as students, and train residents of those communities to run programs in the schools, whether they be after-school sports, arts and computer programs, school-based farms or community improvement initiatives. I would also actively recruit the teaching staff for those schools from people who live in those communities, or communities like them and incorporate the culture and history of the people in those neighborhoods into school curricula.

Right now, the basic thrust of Education Policy™ is making teachers hate teaching, students dread going to school, and parents fear that the love of learning in their children will be snuffed out by excessive testing.

We can do better, but only if our basic goal is to make schools places where young people are inspired and nurtured, and where teaching is treated as a lifetime calling that allows talented people the opportunity to work collaboratively and creatively.

Thank you, Mark. Your ideals are what happen in my dreams when I think of a school system to which kids would want to go.

It sounds so nice, but apparently it's just too difficult. This should be something we get riled up about and fight for. After all the discussions in this book so far, I believe it's time to realize that we are hurting our kids and that we can do better. We've done difficult things before, and we've started from scratch. This time we don't have to do that; we have examples of this type of learning and teaching scattered all over the country in different types of schools in all different types of communities. We have teachers working (and suffocating) in our public schools, who pioneer efforts in inquiry- and project-based learning, as well as the precepts for student-led models like Mark describes. Let's get started.

Schools as Community Centers

I've worked in schools that began using their personnel and resources to offer community programs and assistance—in effect, becoming the community centers of the neighborhoods in which they serve. One fantastic example is Leslie Middle School in Salem, Oregon, a school to which the staff referred as "the hub of the community." Through their own research and conversations with people in their neighborhoods, they concluded that their school population is a microcosm of the area it serves; therefore, it makes creating programs for the community simple, since staff has a good background on the needs of families in the area and can tailor programs accordingly.

With a rapidly growing Hispanic population in Leslie's service area, the staff offered both Spanish and English workshops for reading, writing, and speaking. They offered parenting classes, cooking classes, tax assistance, and financial planning help. They had after-school care, tutoring, open computer labs and library services, and several events throughout the year where students and others could participate in making the neighborhood a better place. Everyone loved it and the students had pride in their school, knowing they spent every day in a building that really made a difference, and in which they had many opportunities to make a difference themselves.

Unfortunately, education budget cuts and redistricting of employees have taken their tolls on these wonderful works. The community liaison no longer works there, class sizes are increasing (one teacher complains of students who need to stand in the back of the room), and crushing standardized testing policies are beginning to take hold in Oregon. Needless to say, in order to make room for the new order of things, the really great things may be put on hold, indefinitely.

This ideal is not hard to accomplish, if schools are allowed to do it. Schools should be funded so that they can serve their communities, as well as students. As noted above, public computer labs, libraries, meeting spaces, fitness centers, and other resources fit perfectly in a public school. Community volunteers are never in short supply, and students would appreciate the convenient venue for community service learning. It seems so logical.

In tight-knit and supportive communities, local businesses are generally happy to sponsor these types of things. In communities where money isn't as freely available, a conversation with the elected leaders is in order. Raising test scores will not fight or end poverty. Providing the nearby schools the resources to act as centers that serve their communities may at least lead to livelier and more engaged kids and parents. College students are more than happy to get involved, as are local business owners who would like to see their neighborhoods begin to revitalize. Turning schools into centers of the community will also give their students the important role of being part of something bigger and necessary.

Letting Kids Learn

I would like to tell you about a recent school observation I did, but first let me just throw out a couple of things about conventional classroom models that make me wonder why we still do them.

Students in desks and tables

I still feel uncomfortable every time I see a classroom full of desks or tables, where each student is assigned a seat and they are expected to remain in that seat unless otherwise instructed. Desks in rows, desks in groups, desks scattered around, even tables where groups of three to four students sit together in teams. Sure, in the real world, it will be necessary to know how to cooperate with other people constructively and collaboratively, but it surely won't look like this, and it's a skill to be developed at a student's own pace.

Desks in rows are just a bad idea. I've been around and around with a few teachers who swear by the continued success of this model. However, it's designed for two things: easy classroom management and making sure students are facing front and listening to lecture. This is a teacher-centric model and is not meant for authentic student learning. I would like to know that we've left this setup in the 1950s to die.

Group arrangements were touted as a great way to get students to talk to each other, learn from each other, and stay occupied on a task while the teacher spent time with each team for further instruction or assistance. These are better than the rows, to be sure, but still have limitations. First, the teacher usually chooses the arrangements; even if students are allowed to pick their own seats, they are still being set up in a prearranged format. Second, the students are generally given a task to work on together to achieve a certain goal or master a given standard, which leads very often (ask any student) to one or two group members doing the bulk of the work and the rest hanging back until they're told to do something. It can be frustrating for the "lead" student, the "following" students, and for the poor teacher, who has to figure out how to grade fairly, yet objectively (remember that working together is not a Common Core standard). I don't think it's always anyone's fault; it's simply an unsustainable and faulty model.

Students are silent and seated

I had an embarrassing moment last year, where a group of my students was talking about the results of an online, standardized practice test they had just taken. I had told them to talk it over, so that they might be able to understand from each other some strategies for doing better. It was bad enough that we were wasting our time and one-to-one technology on that practice, but it got worse when the school counselor came through the door and told my girls that they were being so loud, she could hear them in the hall. I should have closed the door, I suppose, but their noise level was not above normal talk. This has happened often, where in middle school, we are expected to keep our kids quiet, on task, and working bell-to-bell. I have a problem with that, and so should you.

Kids hate being still and quiet and working pencil-to-paper all day, because it's horribly boring and they know they don't learn anything from it. We've already heard the student voice, but it needs to be understood that *teachers* also feel trapped in that silence for fear of being yelled at, embarrassed, or demerited. It happens, and it's wrong. Students should participate, not simply spectate. I often ask adults to imagine themselves in that scenario and how well they could handle sitting still, silent, and focused for 8 hours. Even those of us who have to sit in cubicles have the opportunity to communicate and use some autonomy once in a while.

Work is assigned by the teacher and graded

I know, I know. I've gone off the deep end right? No teacher-assigned work and no grades? Grades are ranks, and little else. Over the past 5 years, I have been in the midst of debates—some of which turned into full-blown screaming matches—about grading scales and procedures, which shows that there is some concern that our traditional 100-point scale just doesn't work anymore. What if there was a place where this all works just fine, and students are growing and prospering in a system that respects their natural cravings for learning and curiosity?

No Desks, No Grades, No Tests

I was recently invited to spend some time at Omni Montessori School, in Charlotte, North Carolina, and see the Montessori model at work. After having seen my conventional environment rapidly deteriorate over five years, and after watching my students become more and more disengaged and nonchalant about their education, this visit almost brought a tear to my eye. Please know that I'm not shilling for or endorsing any particular institution or system (and nobody is paying me or anything), but I saw things happening in Montessori classrooms that I've always used or wanted to try and really want to see in every classroom. Not because they're revolutionary or loudly endorsed or even new. It's because they work, and the students are happy and successful. So, here are my notes from an observation of a late elementary (grades 4-6) classroom:

The campus was misleading to my conventional mind, and I had to ask if I was in the right place. I could see the exterior difference right away. Conventional schools are designed to appear and feel institutional, like a hospital or prison. The Montessori was designed to look like a small neighborhood, with a family of different buildings of different colors, separated by dirt paths, community gardens, bird feeders, and small ponds. It's apparent right away that this place was built with calm discovery in mind, and continues to be a work in progress.

When I walked in, I was greeted by the teacher assistant (TA), who offered me a chair and pointed out the classroom teacher, who was working with two students. There were 27 students in the class, and three of them were in what the TA called a math seminar. A quick survey of the room showed me that there were several different things happening in there at once. I also noticed that there wasn't a single desk in the room, not even for the teacher.

Two boys were reading to each other. A co-ed group of six kids were discussing an essay assignment they were working on and were taking turns reading to each other and listening to critiques. One boy was finishing a math assignment, while two girls nearby were working together on visual aids for a writing assignment. The teacher asked four students to join her at the far side of the room for a paragraph-writing session (for kids who needed extra instruction). And several students were taking part in a pottery lesson, led by a community volunteer.

The noise level was manageable and no one seemed distracted or disturbed. Language among the students was respectful and calm. The teacher didn't have to raise her voice or call attention to a rowdy room (there was a small bell on the wall to bring focus if needed). The students seemed to know what was expected and what they needed to do.

Of course, these kids have gotten used to this type of structure over time—many of them since early childhood. I've seen this type of structure in public school classes, too, before the stricture of the Common Core State Standards squeezed it out and tightened it up. Routines in Montessori schools are very important: mornings are structured to complete required projects and afternoons are more student-directed. Kids are even given a period of time each day to explore their own interests or questions. Math skills are discovered, and then practiced, instead of the traditional other way around. And the importance of community and empathy is consistently reinforced, which is also a trademark of good conventional teachers when they're not mandated to use every Common Core-aligned minute on drills.

Homework is checked twice a week, but isn't graded, at least not in the traditional sense. I watched the TA going through math sheets that she said were brought from home. She said that the parents and students find practice materials at home, complete them, and then bring them to school. The TA then checks their work and looks for mastery, which she defined as "only missing one or two items." If there is a pattern of misunderstanding, she leaves written feedback (not grades or percentages) for the students and parents on how to proceed.

I saw very little technology in this classroom, which I wasn't sure was beneficial or not. Perhaps it was available elsewhere. This was a multi-age group, spanning ages 9 through 12, so perhaps I might see more technology in later grades. But I immediately realized that the respect and collaboration happening trumped the immediate need for technology. Bill Gates would have been very uncomfortable in this classroom.

Finally, students don't take tests at this school. There are no classroom exams or multiple-choice benchmarks. The school, being a public charter, still has to show proficiency against state standards (and the Common Core), but in class, teachers allow students to show that proficiency through authentic assessments. When the end-of-grade exams come around at the end of the year, they are downplayed and their importance is not paramount to anyone's success. Not that it would matter, since I was told that this style of learning never leads to any worry of sanctions by the state. Omni Montessori makes AYP and shows growth every year.

Better Ways to Assess Student Skills

I throw the following phrase around the Internet freely: "There is a better way." That applies to this whole chapter, but let's focus on how we know students are learning and mastering concepts. Standardized tests are lousy indicators of competency and success. Therefore, I would love to see more of the following types of assessments in K-12 school buildings.

Real-Life Challenges[1]

As discussed, kids want to be involved, especially adolescents. When students know that the goal of their learning and hard work is to pass a test, many of them check out because passing a test is not important to them. Give them a real-life challenge where they can use their creativity, their opinions, their backgrounds, their interests, their observational skills, and the help of their peers to truly dig into a modern issue or concern and come up with analyses, understandings, and solutions. The ability to learn a concept or skill and then transfer it to a real-life situation is the foundation of authentic learning and preparation.[2]

It can be a little scary to hand the reigns over to the kids by giving them real-life problems to solve without too much teacher input, but those teachers that have become comfortable with this method will attest to its effectiveness. Remember, kids are still mostly unbiased and untainted by excuses and roadblocks, to which adults continuously turn when faced with hard problems. When a child's unbridled minds are attuned to an issue or problem, their solutions and answers are often brilliant and revolutionary in their simplicity. It takes an adult with years of strict educational discipline to say, "I can't."

Competency-Based Models

I'm a graduate of Western Governors University, a Salt Lake City-based, online university that has won awards for its accessibility and programs. I graduated from the Science Education graduate program with my master's degree, which was an extraordinarily rigorous program. I believe that what made it so rigorous was the fact that the pace and details of the curriculum were based on my own competencies. I was permitted to go as fast as I wanted, into as much depth and analysis as I chose (past certain minimum expectations), and I was required to get my work checked by peers, a mentor, and a third-party grader.

I did not have teachers or instructors. I did not use a textbook. I only took a few standardized tests, which were short and measured objectives that I learned through my own research. If I were to have failed one of those tests, which I didn't, I would have been allowed to see what my strengths and weaknesses were, so that I could review which concepts I had mastered and which I needed to review.

I had the same mentor through the entire program. A mentor is someone who supports you, listens to you, shows you where and how to find resources and help (if needed), and generally stands by you to ensure success. I was never told what to do, when to do it, or told that I had to follow a certain direction. I was allowed to follow my interests in many cases. In cases where I was expected to meet a specific objective, I was allowed to use my creativity and background knowledge to push myself as far into the learning material as I was able. I was not given grades, percentages, or ranks on my records. I either showed mastery or I didn't. If I didn't, I tried again. I graduated when I was able to show mastery across all subjects and during my final capstone project.

So, what is competency-based learning?

Dr. Robert Mendenhall, the president of Western Governors University, says that competency-based education holds a focus on mastery of concepts, rather than the amount of time in school. Students move forward in their education by demonstrating competence in the subject area or content being learned. It is the ultimate *anti*-one-size-fits-all model, since it allows students to individually move at their own paces.[3] After visiting the Montessori school in North Carolina, I saw some bits and pieces of a school that was headed toward competency-based education. At lower ages, kids need more support and "hand holding." However, at the middle school and high school level, it would be beneficial to know that our students are well enough practiced and independent enough to progressively take over their own learning, with the help of a mentor.

Almost every state in the country has a specific number of hours of "seat time" in their law books. It doesn't matter how quickly a student learns, he or she is stuck in "the seat" for that number of hours. There are two problems with this. First, it traps students who have already mastered a subject into a class for the required number of hours, regardless of their ability to show mastery. When that time is up, some students are more than ready to move on, while some students aren't at all ready. Second, it makes true individual learning impossible.

So, why aren't we using competency-based education in public K-12 schools?

Another quick and dirty answer: it's not traditional, which makes it uncomfortable for current practitioners, and it's not the system that the moneymakers in education want to see. Think about the content in this book. One of the biggest benefits of a nationalized and common curriculum for corporate test and textbook publishers, as well as charter schools and private interests, is the ability to sell everyone lots of the same cheap stuff for exorbitant prices. If students were allowed to create their own learning and show mastery in the best way that they and their mentors could conjure, there would be no need for textbooks, and no need for expensive standardized tests. That's the biggest reason. Current budgets are too low to maintain a good mentor system and good resources in the learning communities. This is no accident. This is politics.

Our lawmakers will consistently pass laws and set benchmarks that they remind us, at the top of their lungs, are designed to get every kid "college and career ready." The fact is, there are very few laws that are favorable to our kids' futures. Laws about education are made to favor corporations. It bears repeating.

What about teachers? We were educated and trained to impart knowledge to a listening audience, and then assess them on the things we taught. What if we could simply define mastery for our students, teach them the skills of learning and research, and allow them to progressively become more independent in their learning? It was a very popular movement in the late 1990s and early in the new century. The motto of the progressive education movement was "every year, students should need us less." Why are we afraid of that? Instead of teachers, we would become *mentors*. I love that word. It means that I'm no longer simply a practitioner of content-based teaching, but I am now a practitioner of student-led learning. I think it's an important distinction, and students who have mentors in their lives tend to flourish due to the deep relationships and ongoing support they receive from a few different people for long periods of time.

Ok, so what about assessments? This is where I believe Montessori has the right idea. From what the teacher assistant told me during my visit, it is up to the professional judgment of one to three teachers to determine if a student has mastered a certain concept and may advance. There are no common assessments or standardized tests to determine mastery. If we're truly looking for a scientific way to measure performance and mastery against desired objectives, peer review (yes, teachers should be considered peers; we're all academics, here) is the best method.

There are only a few models of colleges and high schools using competency-based education. The one I'm most familiar with is becoming wildly popular and increasingly successful. Western Governors University has a very high retention rate, compared to other universities, although it has a relatively low graduation rate (which has been attributed to its unusually high rate of students who transfer to other colleges before gaining a degree).[4] Dr. Mendenhall attributes the retention rate to the engagement of the students—they are challenging themselves, rather than waiting for the next assignment, which they may or may not have any interest in.

Let Them Teach!

Omni Montessori is a small school. It has a student profile that is a microcosm of the surrounding community, which is very diverse. It may not be perfect, but it is highly effective for the kids and is a model of progress and student success in life, as well as college and career. Not all schools can be Montessori schools or Western Governors, but why can't they start copying and adjusting the models?

Many public classroom teachers were already teaching like this before they were pressured to stop. Those conventional schoolteachers who taught discovery and inquiry are now the ones who are frustrated and stressed and leaving the profession. When a teacher, who is used to seeing happy kids in his classroom, all of a sudden realizes that he's not permitted to continue proven methods, things turn sour for him and his students. This is the effect of the Common Core Network.

A popular mantra of veteran public school teachers, who know their practice leads their students to success, is "Just let me teach!" They want to stop being quantized and objectified, and watched under a microscope. They want to stop being evaluated by these meaningless test scores and standardized lessons, which have been engineered by corporations that have lost sight of what leads students to learning. Pearson makes a lot of money selling teaching materials to schools, which are tightly aligned (i.e. in partnership) with the Common Core State Standards, and do not lead to understanding or real learning and development. These materials only expose kids to what billionaires want them to know and prepare them to take shallow tests in order to compete against each other.

It's long past time to give the teaching back to the teachers, the leadership of schools back to the principals (rather than state and district accountability offices, which should be restructured or dismantled), and the learning back to the students. Students should be given a voice and a choice in what they learn and how. This is not that hard, and we've done it before. If we can get our schools back in the hands of those who know what they're doing, and those who care about our kids, we may not make our corporate reformers millions of dollars, but we will have successful kids and a more secure nation.

Children of the Core

8

Getting Our Schools Back

"Do what you feel in your heart to be right; for you'll be criticized anyway."

- Eleanor Roosevelt

"Never doubt that a small group of thoughtful, committed citizens can change the world. Indeed, it is the only thing that ever has."

- Margaret Mead

I'd like to briefly summarize some important points before I start talking about what actions we, the parents, can take to keep our kids moving toward a successful and promising future. This list will also help focus on what needs the most attention.

1. Two lawyers developed the Common Core State Standards Initiative, with minimal assistance from

teachers, and with little or no parent or student involvement.

2. The Common Core State Standards are not "fewer, clearer, higher," but are actually more numerous, severely flawed, and stifle critical thinking.

3. Standardized tests, which are increasing every year, are poorly designed, lead to decisions made on "junk science," and cost states and schools approximately $1.7 billion per year - and counting.

4. Students are exhausted, frustrated, and "checking out" of the caustic environment caused by the Common Core Network.

5. Teachers are burning out, and are forced to focus on narrow, dumbed-down skills, in which they don't believe and weren't educated to use.

6. Poor, urban districts are seeing their schools closed and teachers fired because of problems that are caused by poverty and lack of resources.

7. Our kids are growing up in a nation that is being economically and socially weakened by the Common Core Network, and the national and state legislation that enforces it (e.g. Race to the Top).

So, how do we fix this? We keep hearing that it's too late, because the train has left the station. The Common Core Network is already here, in full effect, so how we stop it now?

172

Make Your Own Voice Heard

In January of 2013, teachers in two Seattle high schools risked their jobs and their future career prospects by taking a stand against harmful tests and boycotted the Measures of Academic Progress (MAP) tests that are required by the state several times a year and at great expense. The Garfield and Ballard High School boycotts gained national attention and made plenty of noise on all sides of the education reform debate. The teachers were threatened, the principals were ordered to give the tests anyway, and things were not looking good for them, despite the best efforts from many around the country in their support. The following month, the state legislature voted to suspend the MAP test this year. Why? Because *parents* stood up and showed that they overwhelmingly agree with the teachers and students who were already protesting. We, as parents of public schools, have tremendous power to enact change and support our kids and their teachers.

The Internet is a beautiful thing in times like these. It's so much easier to find things that aren't working (even at great distances) and respond to them. In this chapter, I will talk about many different ways to join the already growing effort to bring our schools back to our kids and teachers, and out of the hands of billionaires and corporate profit-seekers. We hope you join us.

A good place to start is to read the short National Resolution on High-Stakes Testing and sign your endorsement (http://timeoutfromtesting.org/nationalresolution/). This appears to be the largest and fasting growing petition so far.

Once you've done that, get a feel for the local voice by talking with your child's teachers and administrators. Ask some questions. Be polite and cordial, and simply get some information about what they think about the changes in their school. Invite them to discuss the Common Core, standardized tests, and how they use these things in everyday teaching. Ask them how they feel about their environment, the difficulty of their work, and how they are evaluated as teachers. Be a listening ear and a supportive parent; do not come off as an accusatory critic, prowling for mistakes. Ensure their anonymity.

Go to school board meetings. They usually happen once a month, where the public can attend and speak. I invite you to go to one or two, listen to what's being said, and then add your own thoughts. You have three minutes to speak your mind. Go!

Then, use your social networking prowess. There are dozens of groups on Facebook, Twitter and Google+, where parents, students, and teachers are organizing and planning their strategies and assisting each other through problems and trials. Look for the following groups, which always welcome new members (an asterisk * means that the group also has several state-specific groups):

1. Parents Across America*
(parentsacrossamerica.org)
2. Save Our Schools*

(saveourschoolsmarch.org)

3. United Opt Out: The National Movement
    (unitedoptout.com)

4. Opt Out of Standardized Tests Wiki*
    (optoutofstandardizedtests.wikispaces.com)

5. FairTest.org

6. Parents United
    (parentsunited.org)

All of these groups also have Facebook pages, where discussions and ideas are happening every day. Get involved with one or all, especially where people from your state are involved.

While I'm pointing out groups to pay attention to and join with, let me point to a few that you should pay attention to, but with a critical mind. The following groups call themselves "grassroots" and "parent-powered," but they are simply corporate-sponsored propaganda mouthpieces. There is nothing grassroots about these groups, and they are responsible for the task of pushing the Common Core Network into every school, with the ultimate goal of complete corporate takeover of public schools (asterisk * means the same thing as before):

1. StudentsFirst*
    (studentsfirst.org)

2. Democrats for Education Reform
    (dfer.org)

3. Students for Education Reform*

(studentsforedreform.org)

4. Parent Revolution (these are not parents)
   (parentrevolution.org)

It's often easy to tell the difference. The first list wants your voice and perhaps a donation. The second list generally wants your money so that they can increase their lobbying power.

Then, speak to your fellow parents. Let them know how you feel. Share stories about your children in school and during testing. Be a voice of reason and change, and help get our dormant parent force moving again. We've done it before. You may get some blank stares and even some resistance, but keep talking. You will find many parents who share the frustration.

As cliché as it may sound, write a letter! There is an ongoing letter-writing campaign directed at President Obama, where teachers are organized by state to send a letter and make a phone call to the White House every week. Join the effort with your own voice. To get ideas and support, look for the Facebook pages, "Teachers' Letters to Obama" and "Dump Duncan." Make sure you write letter after letter after letter (and emails) to your local representatives, school board members, and superintendents as well.

Stop Participating—Opt Out of Standardized Tests

There is no violent revolution here. There is no screaming or fighting or loud protest necessary on your part. The most effective way to change the bad direction of our education system right now is silent, peaceful resistance. Dr. Martin Luther King, Jr., Mahatma Gandhi, and other peaceful revolutionaries fought injustice by simply refusing to participate in the systems in which they lived. And they got others to do the same. This is the most important step in this movement of resistance. When parents stick up for their kids against government control, things start to change. Indeed, they have already started to change.

In order to stop standardized testing, it's going to take a large and coordinated action by many parents across many states. The nice thing is, it's easy for one person to start. Others will follow. It's already started, so you aren't going to be alone. Of course, we are stronger in numbers, so, after talking to other parents, try to find some friends who will join your plight. Try this:

Write a letter to the district, school, or state leadership politely informing them that your child(ren) will no longer be participating in high-stakes standardized tests, which are used to rank or evaluate children or teachers. Remember, you are not *requesting*, you are *informing*. Give them some valid reasons, such as your religious, medical, philosophical, or political opposition to these tests. So far, there is no state that can penalize you for opting your child out, although you may hear some school personnel use scare tactics. There are some states that will attempt to penalize your child, and I'll get to that in the next subheading. Visit the *Opt Out of Standardized Tests Wiki* to learn more about policies in your state. Then, visit *United Opt*

Out to see advice on how to proceed. Finally, join an opt-out group on Facebook to get support and share your successes and challenges (see the *Further Reading and Resources* page at the end of the book).

Remember, this is for your child and your child's future. It will also lead to the brighter futures of other children. And there are many, many of us out there who are waiting and excited to help you. When other parents see that more and more of us are taking this action to support and protect our own kids, they will follow suit. There will be a critical mass, if we make it happen, where the bubble will burst.

Report Violations to Your Rights

If you are threatened with legal action or if your child is threatened with retention, denial of grade advancement, or failing, *get everything in writing*, and then contact the following advocates:

> **American Civil Liberties Union (ACLU) Multi Family Complaint**
>
> *The ACLU is accumulating letters regarding state testing, where schools/states have violated the rights of parents to guide their child's education. The U.S. Supreme Court supports a parent's right to guide their child's education as an 'unwritten liberty,' protected by the Due Process Clause of the Fourteenth Amendment.*

If you want to participate, write a hard copy letter containing:

- *An overview of your story*
- *Threatening letters / email or denials to school activities, graduation, and grade advancement*
- *Permission to join in on the ACLU complaint*
- *Your return address*
- *Your signature*

Submit to: Nina Bishop

3065 Windward Way

Colorado Springs, CO 80917

Questions: 719-233-1508

Students who are on IEPs or 504s have specific guidelines for how instruction and assessment must be modified or what accommodations the school must meet, including opting out of state standardized tests. If your child's special needs guidelines are being violated by the instruction or testing happening in school, try bringing your concerns to the following people, in this order:

1. Talk to your child's teacher or teaching team.
2. Talk to the principal
3. Talk to the school or district's 504 or IEP coordinator
4. Contact the U.S. Department of Education Civil Rights Department.

If your concern is not satisfactorily addressed, contact the ACLU or local education rights advocates. It may even be beneficial to contact an education lawyer if you believe that individual human rights have been violated; several of them work *pro bono* for cases like these.

Join Your Local Teacher Protest

The news has been alive lately with gatherings, protests, marches, and sit-ins in cities around the country, where teachers and school staff have patiently awaited the audience of education and government leaders. There is a special type of contempt in our government these days, where leaders don't feel it necessary to address their constituents anymore, but it does make news, especially when the noise is constant and others share the message.

A small district outside of Buffalo, New York, has its own boycott, in which teachers refuse to submit unfair evaluation plans to the state department of education, which they feel hurt students and punish teachers. The state will only approve evaluation plans that are based largely on student test scores. The teachers and administrators of that district will not succumb to unfair practices, regardless of the consequences.

There have been teacher strikes already in Chicago and large protests in Wisconsin, Oregon, Michigan, Illinois, Indiana, New York, California, and other states, where testing, Common Core, unfair evaluations, and school closings have begun to show how dangerous the corporate reform movement can be. The Common Core Network is no longer a silent coup, operating under our radar. We are bringing the dirty deeds to light, and we need our parents to start to look closely, ask questions, and stand up for their kids.

I invite you to join them. If nothing else, it will help you get a real feel for how fiercely our teachers are fighting for our kids. The media likes to paint teachers as selfish union thugs who are crying about their wages. The truth is, teachers always put children first. Your presence and support will also give teachers (and you) a feeling of community and solidarity as we all show our resolve in standing up for our kids.

Keep Kids in the Loop

I think the most important thing to remember is to keep our children involved with what's happening to their education. Talk about it constructively and openly with them, without too much anger and without vitriol. Let them open up and listen to what they've heard or how they feel about school and about the things they're learning. If they're bored, ask them why. If they're stressed or frustrated, find out why. Don't jump to the conclusions of ADD or behavior issues right away. As one of my friends says, "Your kids don't need pills to keep them focused;

they need a stimulating curriculum and an environment where they can spread their intellectual wings."

Allow your children to talk to each other about their school life. There are student voice chapters popping up in several universities with the goal of educating high school students about the Common Core Network. Middle school and high school students want to discuss their frustrations with those who will listen, and I hope that their parents are the first go-to people, followed by these peers. Adolescents also need to be part of the solution. If children see an action that is productive and nondestructive, we must let them take it. Encourage your kids to write letters, blog, speak at board meetings, host discussion parties, and use whatever creative media they wish to get their voices out. This is how we should be schooling them also, incidentally.

Our High-Stakes Resolution

Even as we think about the importance of a strong public education system for our country, we all carry our own stake in the process and the outcomes: our kids. Education is the foundation for our nation's economic success, global position in the next-generation knowledge economy, our technological standing, our democratic freedoms, our scientific progress, and our national security. All of those are currently at risk, by the hands of corporate entities that are looking simply at how to rank, file, and stratify the citizens of the United States to their own benefit. To be blunt, this is class warfare at its most basic, and the top 1% has the upper hand. But we can and will turn the tables.

Nationalizing education and setting it up to become a profit machine is an aggressive move, which has been done in other countries before. The outcome is never desirable for the citizens of those countries. The middle class shrinks, labor is controlled by the super-wealthy, jobs are low-wage and unskilled, and social programs are gutted, creating an expansion in poverty and hunger. When a small club of billionaires controls education and wealth, the national economy stagnates while inflation rises and wages stall. The currency loses value and the economy of the United States on the world stage will be in more trouble than it is.

I wish I could say that this is all just alarmism, but I can't. It's happened before, like I said. The social experiments we're seeing in the last decade are not revolutionary and have ended badly in the past. Just because we're America doesn't mean it will end differently for us. We're already seeing the negative effects in our current child poverty rates and job markets. Student debt is over a trillion dollars, cumulatively, and working class citizens are in hock for billions of dollars. We already owe our lives to banks and now we are offering our kids to those same people.

That's what we really care about. Our kids are in trouble. Not only are they losing their motivation, engagement, and their precious gifts of creativity and learning through play and collaboration; they are also losing the right to be successful, regardless of their background. Arne Duncan calls education "the civil rights issue" of our time, at the same that his policies, in conjunction with the Common Core Network, are ensuring the systematic burial of our kids' futures.

As usual, the damage is worse as we go down the socioeconomic scale. Affluent students who attend well-funded public and private schools are barely feeling the effects of the corporate grab, since these students have already been chosen as the future's elite. Poorer, urban students are seeing themselves labeled as failing, their schools are being closed, their teachers are being fired, and their new schools are run like military institutions and prisons. This truly is a civil rights issue, and we are watching it happen, clueless and helpless.

This can't happen any longer. These are our children.

They are not commodities. They are not to be traded on the stock market.

They are not test scores. They cannot be measured by Bill Gates-style objective measures. They cannot be ranked and filed by achievement scores for the purposes of widening corporate profit margins. They should not be sitting in test preparation factories for 8 hours per day, trying their hardest to stay focused and out of trouble.

They are not prisoners or military cadets. They cannot be shushed and contained within narrow intellectual confines and concrete walls.

They are not products. They cannot be shuffled from building to building, when their government decides they are not creating a good enough return-on-investment.

They are not guinea pigs. They do not deserve to be placed into the social experiments of Michelle Rhee, Arne Duncan, ALEC, and the billionaire foundations that wish to try their best indoctrination techniques on the impressionable and mostly helpless portion of the population.

The bottom line is, these are our kids. It doesn't matter where we come from, how much money we make, what part of town we live in, how highly educated we are, what type of car we drive, how important our job is, what our last name is, what color our skin is, or anything else. We love our kids. We cherish them. We want to see them smile, and play, and look at the sky in wonder, and ask questions, and treat each other with love and respect. We don't want them to become sterile, unthinking, and obedient automatons of an overactive, corporate-driven system that hopes to classify them by their abilities to rote memorize facts, follow orders, work obediently, and accept their fates.

What we really want is for our children to grow to love their places in the world and the learning that can happen every day with the right guidance and time. Our schools should look and feel much different than they did when we were kids, and they should certainly not look like the test-prep factories we see today. The hallways of our schools should echo with the sounds of discovery, fun, play, discussions, debates, excitement, questions, more questions, and community. Schools should be places where our students go to explore their interests and their curiosities, and where highly educated adults become mentors and facilitators of those learning journeys. Schools should be communities of thinkers and doers, who act in the interest of those communities and work together to make their learning meaningful and powerful.

When our kids graduate from these learning communities, we want them to be freethinking and contributing members of their society. We want them to be prepared to truly participate in their own broader communities, whether college or career or anywhere else. We hope they will be prepared to make a real difference in how their nation is perceived and interacted with on the global stage, which will bring us all security, health, and economic progress. Our kids, in addition to the most precious things in our lives, are the collective bridge to a future where we need them to be more creative, more progressive, and more sharing than we have ever been before. That means it's time to stop the one-size-fits-all and punitive workings of the Common Core Network.

This is up to us, the parents and teachers and students. We are the only group large enough, scary enough, and powerful enough to truly make the change we want to see for our kids.

Teachers and education experts have begun the fight and are paving the way for us. It's our turn to make our voices heard. There is one mighty weapon that is much more powerful than the money that's being used to jeopardize our kids' futures: our love and hope for our children.

Children of the Core

FURTHER READING AND RESOURCES

Common Core Blogs
1. *Education without Representation*. Christel Lane Swasey. http://whatiscommoncore.wordpress.com/
2. *Teaching the Core*. Dave Stuart. http://www.teachingthecore.com/
3. *Diane Ravitch's Blog* (Common Core Category). Diane Ravitch. http://dianeravitch.net/category/common-core/
4. *Education in the Age of Globalization*. Yong Zhao. http://zhaolearning.com/category/blog/
5. *Change the Stakes*. http://changethestakes.org
6. *First, Do No Harm*. Kris L. Nielsen. http://atthechalkface.com/category/kris-nielsen-first-do-no-harm/
7. *CCSSI Mathematics*. http://ccssimath.blogspot.com/

Education Reform Watch Blogs
1. *Susan Ohanian Speaks Out*. Susan Ohanian. http://susanohanian.org/
2. *NYC Public School Parents*. http://nycpublicschoolparents.blogspot.com/?m=1
3. *Living in Dialogue*. Anthony Cody. http://blogs.edweek.org/teachers/living-in-dialogue/

4. *The IDEA Blog*. Institute for Democratic Education in America.
   http://democraticeducation.org/index.php/blog/
5. The National Center for Fair and Open Testing.
   http://fairtest.org/
6. *Yinzercation*. Jessie Ramey, Ph.D.
   http://yinzercation.wordpress.com/
7. *GFBrandenburg's Blog*.
   http://gfbrandenburg.wordpress.com/
8. *Jersey Jazzman*. http://jerseyjazzman.blogspot.com/
9. *Edushyster.com*. http://edushyster.com/
10. *Fred Klonsky's Blog*. Fred Klonsky.
    http://preaprez.wordpress.com/
11. *Ms. Katie's Ramblings*. Katie Osgood.
    http://mskatiesramblings.blogspot.com/
12. *The Frustrated Teacher*. Richard Sugerman.
    http://www.thefrustratedteacher.com/
13. *With a Brooklyn Accent*. Mark Naison.
    http://withabrooklynaccent.blogspot.com/
14. *At the Chalk Face*. http://atthechalkface.com/

Education News and Updates
1. *Washington Post's The Answer Sheet*. Valerie Strauss.
   http://www.washingtonpost.com/blogs/answer-sheet/
2. *Deborah Meier on Education*. Deborah Meier.
   http://deborahmeier.com/

3. *Schools Matter.* http://www.schoolsmatter.info/

Specific Education Concerns and Organizations
1. *Class Size Matters.* Leonie Haimson.
   http://www.classsizematters.org/
2. *Teacher Under Construction.* Stephanie Rivera.
   http://teacherunderconstruction.com/

Models of Education Sites
1. *BuildBetterSchools.* Conny Jensen.
   http://www.buildbetterschools.com/
2. *Montessori Madness.* Trevor Eissler.
   http://www.montessorimadness.com/

Important Books to Read
1. *The Death and Life of the Great American School System: How Testing and Choice are Undermining Education.* Diane Ravitch. Basic Books, 2011.
2. *One Size Does Not Fit All.* Nikhil Goyal. Bravura Books, 2012.
3. *Free Voluntary Reading.* Stephen Krashen. Libraries Unlimited, 2011.
4. *The Power of Their Ideas: Lessons for America from a Small School in Harlem.* Deborah Meier. Beacon Press, 2002.

5. *Tested: One American School Struggles to Make the Grade*. Linda Perlstein. Holt Paperbacks, 2008.

NOTES

INTRODUCTION

1. United Opt Out: The National Movement, "I Quit." 2012.
http://unitedoptout.com/i-quit/

2. Line Dalile, "How Schools are Killing Creativity."
Huffington Post. April 9, 2012.
http://www.huffingtonpost.com/line-dalile/a-dictator-
racing-to-nowh_b_1409138.html

3. The Conference Board, "Are They Really Ready to Work?"
2013.
http://www.conferenceboard.org/publications/publicationde
tail.cfm?publicationid=1218

4. Dana Goldstein, "On David Coleman, 'Life Writing,' and
the Future of the American Reading List." May 17, 2012.
http://www.danagoldstein.net/dana_goldstein/2012/05/on-
david-coleman-life-writing-and-the-future-of-the-american-
reading-list.html

College Board, "Our President." 2013. http://about.College
Board.org/leadership/president

CHAPTER 1

1.   Robert Marzano and Jana Marzano, "The Keys to Classroom Management." ASCD. September 2003. http://www.ascd.org/publications/educational-leadership/sept03/vol61/num01/The-Key-to-Classroom-Management.aspx

2.   Kris L. Nielsen, "Why the SMART Board May Have Been a Dumb Choice." Middle Grades Mastery. April 15, 2012. http://mgmfocus.com/2012/04/15/why-the-smart-board-may-have-been-a-dumb-choice/

3.   Tom Bigda-Peyton, "The Problem of Education." An Economy of Meaning. September 20, 2010. http://aneconomyofmeaning.wordpress.com/2010/09/20/%E2%80%9Cthe-problem-of-education-can-a-19th-century-model-succeed-in-a-21st-century-world%E2%80%9D/

4.   Common Core State Standards Initiative, "Mathematics." http://www.corestandards.org/Math

5.   Jeff Dunn, "How Do We Prepare Students for Jobs That Don't Yet Exist?" Edudemic. October 25, 2011. http://edudemic.com/2011/10/students-of-the-future/

CHAPTER 2

1.   Diane Ravitch, "The Conservative Case Against Common Core." July 22, 2012.

http://dianeravitch.net/2012/07/22/the-conservative-case-against-the-common-core-standards/

2. Jacob E. Adams Jr., "Education Reform."

http://education.stateuniversity.com/pages/1944/Education-Reform.html

3. Erik Kain, "The Deep Pockets Behind Education Reform." *Forbes.* May 25, 2011.

http://www.forbes.com/sites/erikkain/2011/05/25/the-deep-pockets-behind-education-reform/

4. Tamar Lewin, "Many States Adopt National Standards for Their Schools." July 21, 2010.

http://www.nytimes.com/2010/07/21/education/21standards.html?_r=0

CHAPTER 3

1. Columbia University Teachers College "What is Big Business' Interest in Education?" October 1, 1998.
http://www.tc.columbia.edu/news.htm?articleID=2205&pub=6&issue=24

2. Jonathan Rabinovitz, "Poor Ranking on International Test Misleading About U.S. Performance." Stanford Report. January 15, 2013.

http://news.stanford.edu/news/2013/january/test-scores-ranking-011513.html

3. Valerie Strauss, "A New Look at Teach for America." *The Washington Post.* July 11, 2010.

http://voices.washingtonpost.com/answer-sheet/teachers/a-new-look-at-teach-for-americ.html

4.   Common Core State Standards Initiative, "Frequently Asked Questions." 2012.
http://www.corestandards.org/resources/frequently-asked-questions

5.   Scott Foresman, "Reading Street: Envision It Handbook." 2011. Pearson Publishing. ISBN: 978-0-328-4563-8.

6.   Michael Morella, "Common Core Standards: Early Results from Kentucky Are In." *U.S. News*. December 4, 2012.
http://www.usnews.com/opinion/articles/2012/12/04/common-core-standards-early-results-from-kentucky-are-in

7.   Columbia University Teachers College "What is Big Business' Interest in Education?" October 1, 1998.
http://www.tc.columbia.edu/news.htm?articleID=2205&pub=6&issue=24

CHAPTER 4

1.   Alice Rivlin, *Systematic Thinking for Social Action*. July 19, 1971. Brooking Institute Press.

2.   National Center for Education Statistics, "Report in Brief: NAEP 1994 Trends in Academic Progress." October 1996.
http://nces.ed.gov/nationsreportcard/pubs/main1994/97583.asp

3. Federal Education Budget Project, "Background & Analysis." *New America Foundation.* September 12, 2012. http://febp.newamerica.net/background-analysis/no-child-left-behind-overview

4. Noliwe M. Rooks, "Why It's Time to Get Rid of Standardized Tests." *Time.* October 11, 2012. http://ideas.time.com/2012/10/11/why-its-time-to-get-rid-of-standardized-tests/

5. W. James Popham, "Why Standardized Tests Don't Measure Educational Quality." *Educational Leadership.* March 1999. http://www.ascd.org/publications/educational-leadership/mar99/vol56/num06/Why-Standardized-Tests-Don't-Measure-Educational-Quality.aspx

6. Holly Ramer, "Dartmouth College Ending Advanced Placement Credit." *Huffington Post.* January 17, 2013. http://www.huffingtonpost.com/2013/01/17/dartmouth-college-ending-_0_n_2496662.html

7. Jem Muldoon, "Concerns About Online Assessment? Yes! It's CAT." *In Search of Hecuba's Torch.* January 12, 2013. http://jemmuldoon.blogspot.com/2013/01/concerns-about-online-assessment-yes.html?m=1

8. NYC Public School Parents, "Parents Beware!" January 18, 2013. http://nycpublicschoolparents.blogspot.com/2013/01/parents-beware-ny-and-eight-other.html?m=1

CHAPTER 5

1.   *Students' names have been changed for anonymity.*

2.   Nikhil Goyal, *One Size Does Not Fit All*. September 5, 2012. Bravura Books.

3.   Stephen Krashen, "Is In-school Free Reading Good for Children?" http://www.sdkrashen.com/articles/in-school%20FVR/all.html

CHAPTER 6

1.   Stephanie Simon, "Privatizing Public Schools: Big Firms Eyeing Profits from U.S. K-12 Market." *Huffington Post*. August 2, 2012. http://www.huffingtonpost.com/2012/08/02/private-firms-eyeing-prof_n_1732856.html

2.   Alyssa Granacki, "Poverty is Not Destiny: Demanding Change for the Future." *Huffington Post*. August 29, 2012. http://www.huffingtonpost.com/alyssa-granacki/poverty-education_b_1837469.html *"Poverty is Not Destiny" is the rally cry of Teach for America, whose philosophy is that raising the bar (and test scores) will pull children out of poverty.*

3.   National Center for Children in Poverty, "Child Poverty." http://www.nccp.org/topics/childpoverty.html

4.   Lisa Wade, "The Correlation Between Income and SAT Scores." *The Society Pages*. August 29, 2012. http://thesocietypages.org/socimages/2012/08/29/the-correlation-between-income-and-sat-scores/

5.   Diane Ravitch, "Bill Gates and the Cult of Measurement." January 31, 2013. http://dianeravitch.net/2013/01/31/bill-gates-and-the-cult-of-measurement/

6.   Anthony Cody, "Gerald Coles: KIPP Schools: Power Over Evidence." *Education Week*. August 15, 2012. http://blogs.edweek.org/teachers/living-in-dialogue/2012/08/gerald_coles_kipp_schools_powe.html

7.   G.F. Brandenburg, "Poverty isn't Destiny?" http://gfbrandenburg.wordpress.com/2013/01/21/poverty-isnt-destiny/

8.   American Civil Liberties Union, "What is the School-to-Prison Pipeline?" http://www.aclu.org/racial-justice/what-school-prison-pipeline

CHAPTER 7

1.   Adapted from "9 Ways to Assess Without Standardized Tests," by Lisa Michelle Nielsen. *The Innovative Educator*. April 22, 2012. http://theinnovativeeducator.blogspot.com/2012/04/8-ways-to-assess-without-standardized.html

2.   Annie Murphy Paul, "What is Transfer? And Why is it So Hard to Achieve?" *The Brilliant Blog*. February 12, 2013. http://anniemurphypaul.com/2013/02/what-is-transfer-and-why-is-it-so-hard-to-achieve/#

3.   Robert Mendenhall, "What is Competency-Based Education?" *Huffington Post*. September 5, 2012.

http://www.huffingtonpost.com/dr-robert-
mendenhall/competency-based-learning-_b_1855374.html
*Incidentally, Dr. Mendenhall is the president of my alma
mater, Western Governors University.*
4.   American School Search, "Western Governors University
- Review and Ranking." http://www.american-school-
search.com/review/western-governors-university

For more information on the movement to end the corporate education reform systems currently in place, kindly visit the following companion website:

www.childrenofthecore.com

To schedule the author for a speaking engagement at your school, community event, or other conference, please email klnielsen74@gmail.com.

In solidarity,

Kris L. Nielsen

ABOUT THE AUTHOR

Kris L. Nielsen has been a middle grades educator and instructional leader for six years in New Mexico, Oregon, and North Carolina. He is a graduate of Western Governors University's Master of Science Education program, with emphasis on child development and instructional technology. Kris is an activist against corporate education reform and has had his writing featured in several online magazines and blogs, including those of the *Washington Post* and Diane Ravitch. He currently blogs at www.atthechalkface.com. Kris lives in New York State with his two daughters, young son, and beautiful wife.